Felix Vallotton:
168 Paintings and Drawings

By Maria Tsaneva

First Edition

*****

I0474559

Felix Vallotton: 168 Paintings and Drawings
*****

Foreword

Félix Edouard Vallotton (1865 – 1925) was a Swiss painter and printmaker associated with Les Nabis.

He was born into a conservative middle-class family in Lausanne, and there he attended Collège Cantonal, graduating with a degree in classical studies in 1882. In that year he moved to Paris to study art under Jules Joseph Lefebvre and Gustave Boulanger at the Académie Julian. He spent many hours in the Louvre, where he greatly admired the works of Holbein, Dürer and Ingres; these artists would remain exemplars for Vallotton throughout his life. Vallotton's earliest paintings, chiefly portraits, are firmly rooted in the academic tradition.

During the following decade Vallotton painted, wrote art criticism and made a number of prints. In 1891 he executed his first woodcut, a portrait of Paul Verlaine. The many woodcuts he produced during the 1890s were recognized as innovative, and established Vallotton as a leader in the revival of true woodcut as an artistic medium. Vallotton emphasized outline and flat patterns, and generally eliminated the gradations and modeling traditionally produced by hatching. He was influenced by post-Impressionism, Symbolism, and especially by the Japanese woodcut: a large exhibition of ukiyo-e prints had been presented at the École des Beaux-Arts in 1890, and Vallotton, like many artists of his era an enthusiast of Japonism, collected these prints.

His woodcut subjects included domestic scenes, bathing women, portrait heads, and several images of street crowds and demonstrations. He usually depicted types rather than individuals. Vallotton's graphic art reached its highest development in Intimités (Intimacies), a series of ten interiors published in 1898 by the Revue Blanche, which deal with tension between men and women.Vallotton's woodcuts were widely disseminated in periodicals and books in Europe as well as in the United States, and have been suggested as a significant influence on the graphic art of Edvard Munch, Aubrey Beardsley, and Ernst Ludwig Kirchner.

By 1892 he was affiliated with Les Nabis, a group of young artists that included Pierre Bonnard, Ker-Xavier Roussel, Maurice Denis, and Edouard Vuillard, with whom Vallotton was to form a lifelong friendship. During the 1890s, when Vallotton was closely allied with the avant-garde, his paintings reflected the style of his woodcuts, with flat areas of color, hard edges, and simplification of detail. His subjects included genre scenes, portraits and nudes.

In 1899 Vallotton married Gabrielle Rodrigues-Henriques, a wealthy young widow with three children, and in 1900 he attained French citizenship. Around 1899, his printmaking activity diminished as he concentrated on painting, developing a sober, often bitter realism independently of the artistic mainstream.

Vallotton's paintings of the post-Nabi period found admirers, and were generally respected for their truthfulness and their technical qualities, but the severity of his style was frequently criticized. Typical is the reaction of the critic who, writing in the March 23, 1910 issue of Neue Zürcher Zeitung, complained that Vallotton "paints like a policeman, like someone whose job it is to catch forms and colors. Everything creaks with an intolerable dryness ... the colors lack all joyfulness." In its uncompromising character his art prefigured the New Objectivity that flourished in Germany during the 1920s, and has a further parallel in the work of Edward Hopper.

He continued to publish occasional art criticism, in addition to other writings. He wrote eight plays, some of which received performances, although their reviews appear to have been unfavorable.He also wrote three novels, including the semi-autobiographical La Vie meurtrière (The Murderous Life).

Vallotton responded in 1914 to the coming of the First World War by volunteering for the French army, but he was rejected because of his age. In 1915–16 he returned to the medium of woodcut for the first time since 1901 to express his feelings for his adopted country in the series, This is War, his last prints. He subsequently spent three weeks on a tour of the Champagne front in 1917, on a commission from the Ministry of Fine Arts. The sketches he produced became the basis for a group of paintings in which he recorded with cool detachment the ruined landscape. In his last years Félix Vallotton concentrated especially on still lifes and on "composite landscapes", landscapes composed in the studio from memory and imagination. Always a prolific artist, by the end of his life he had completed over 1700 paintings and about 200 prints, in addition to hundreds of drawings and several sculptures. He died on the day after his 60th birthday, following cancer surgery in Paris in 1925.

Paintings and Drawings

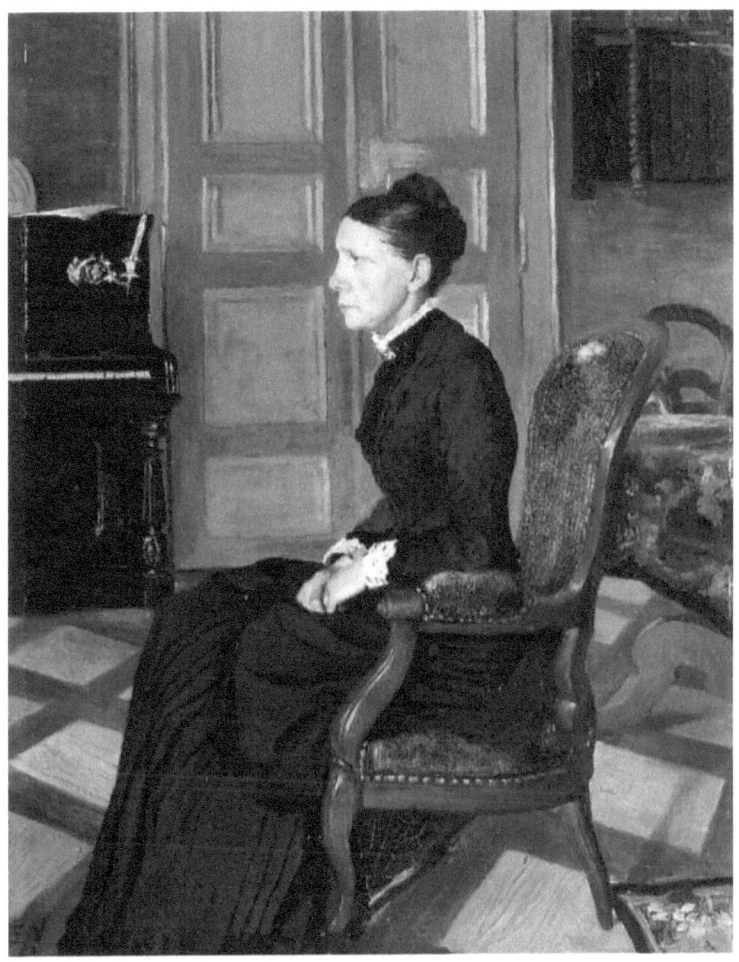

The Artist`s Mother, 1884, oil on canvas

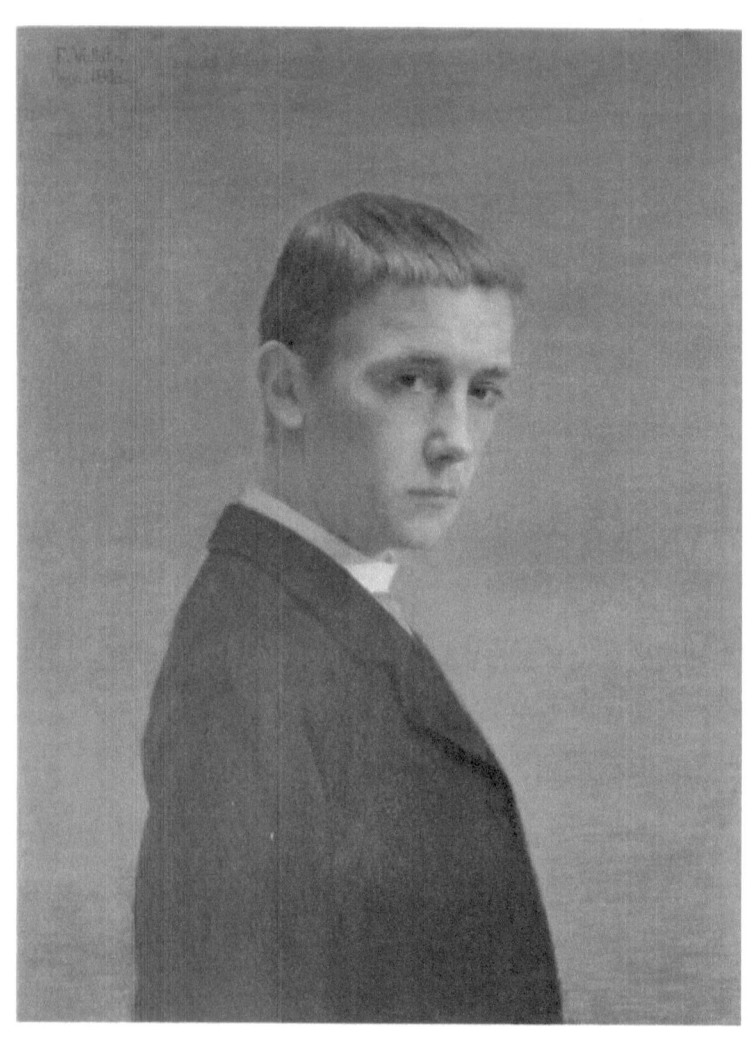

My portrait, 1885, oil on canvas

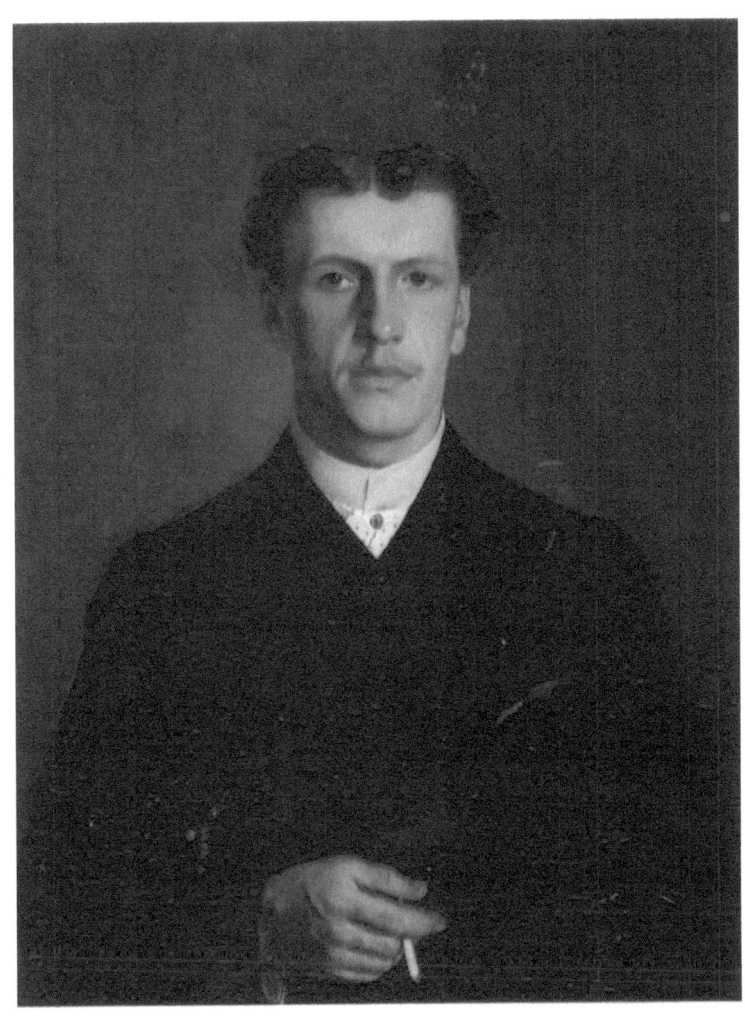

Paul Vallotton, the Artist`s Brother, 1886, oil on canvas

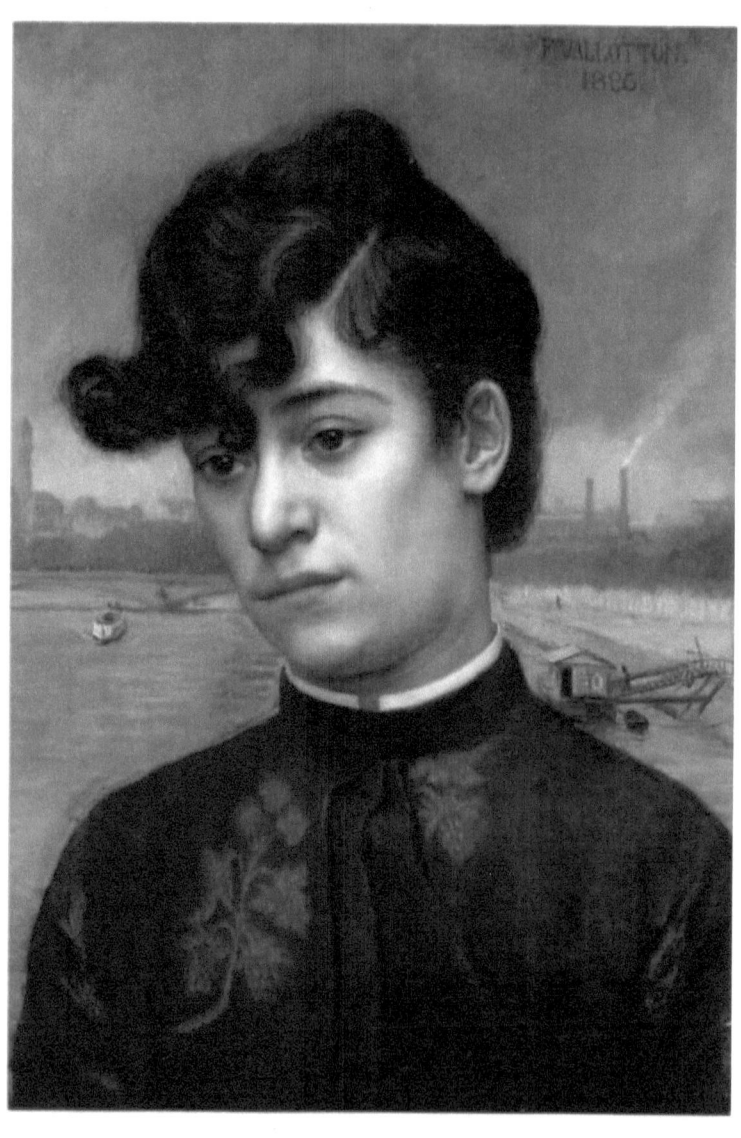

Portrait of Juliette Lacour (model), 1886, oil on canvas

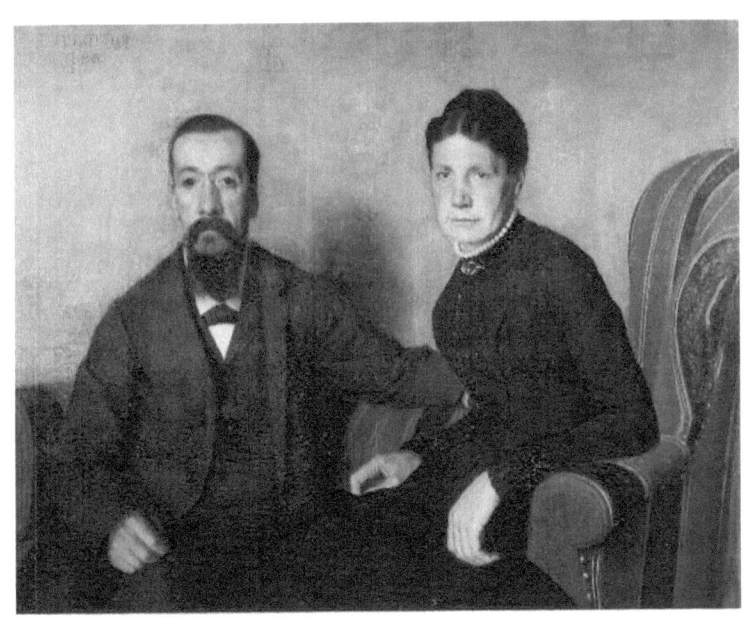

The Artist`s Parents, 1886, oil on canvas

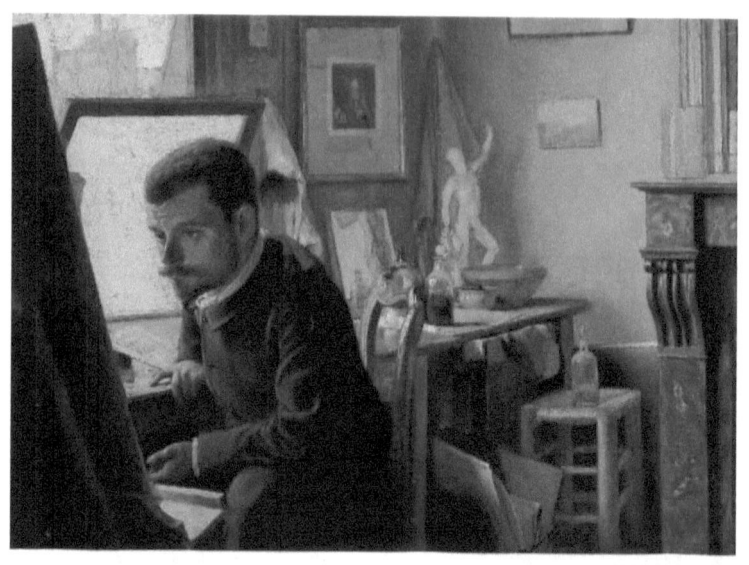

Felix Jasinski in His Printmaking Studio, 1887, oil on canvas

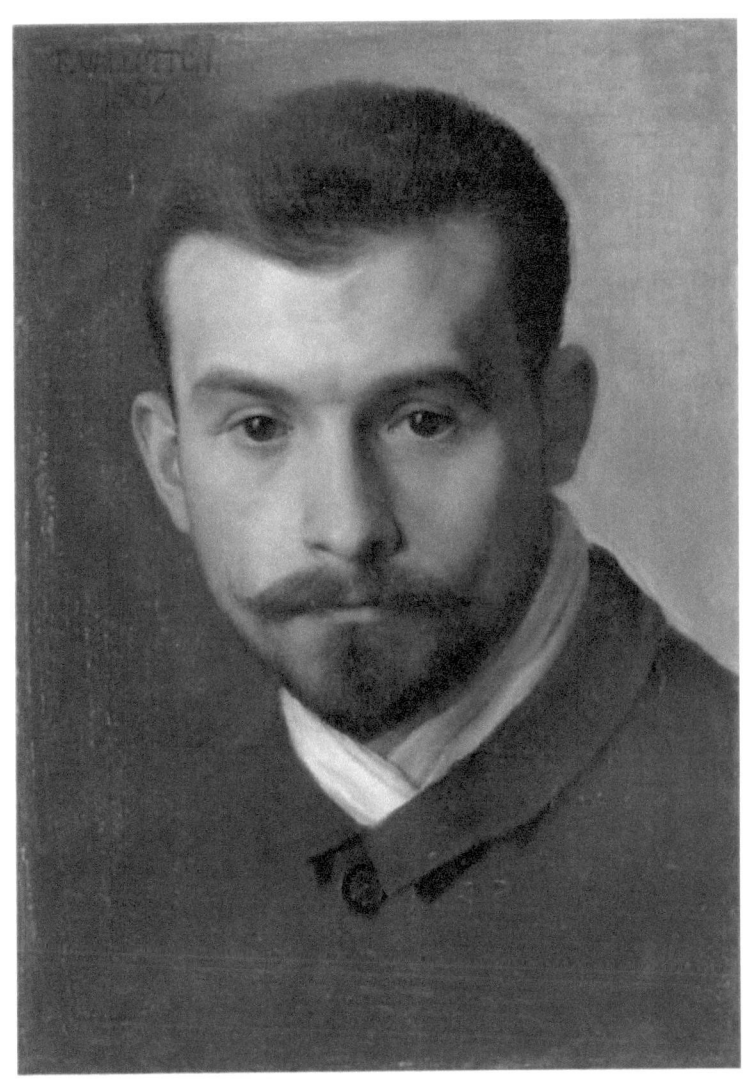

Félix Stanislas Jasinski, 1887, oil on canvas

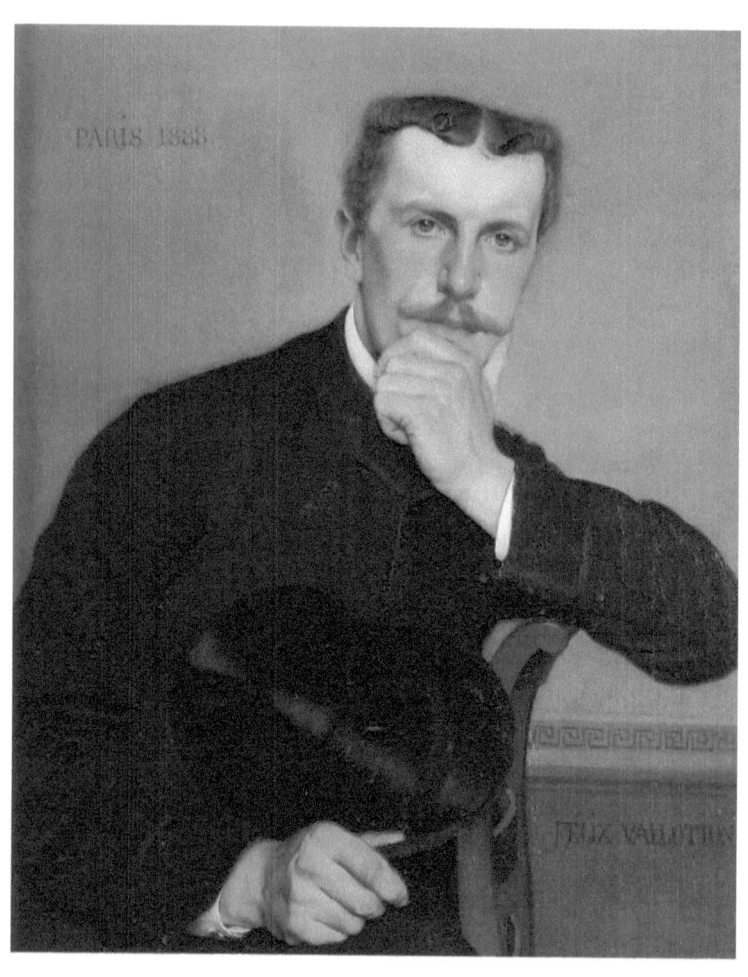

Portrait of the Artist`s Brother with Hat, 1888, oil on canvas

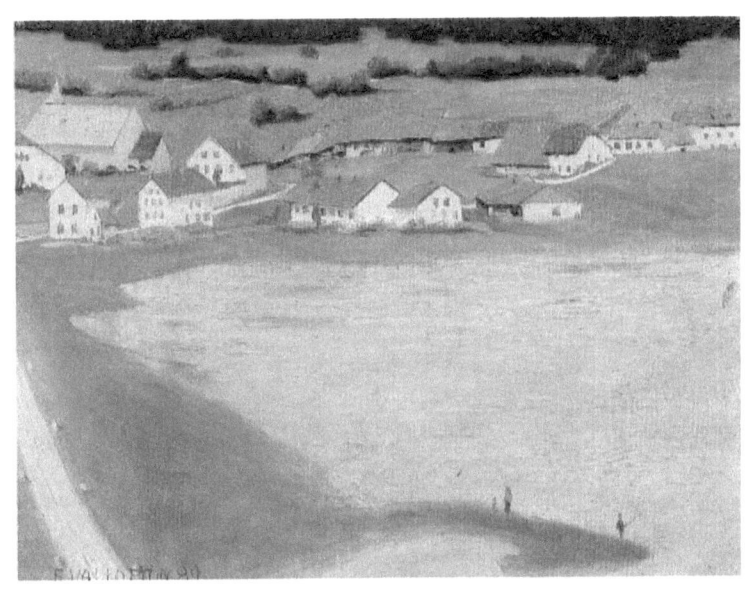

The Coal Scuttles, 1889, oil on canvas

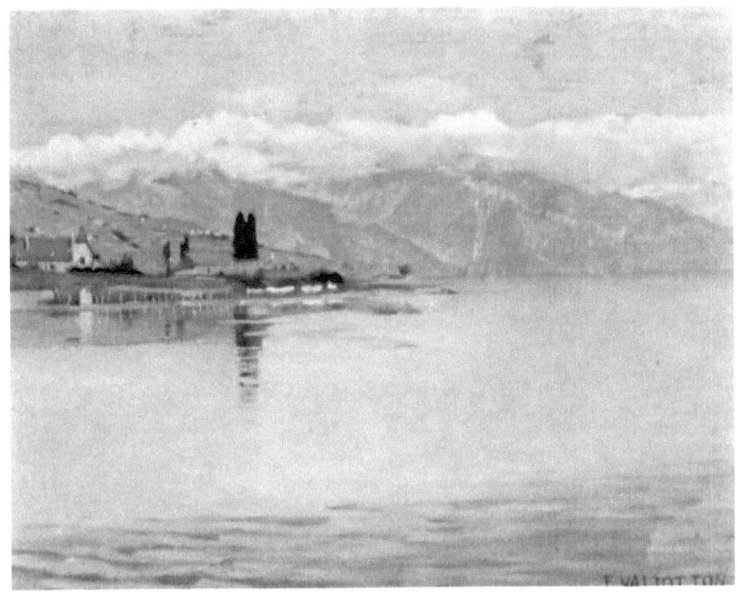

The port of Pully (study), 1889, oil on canvas

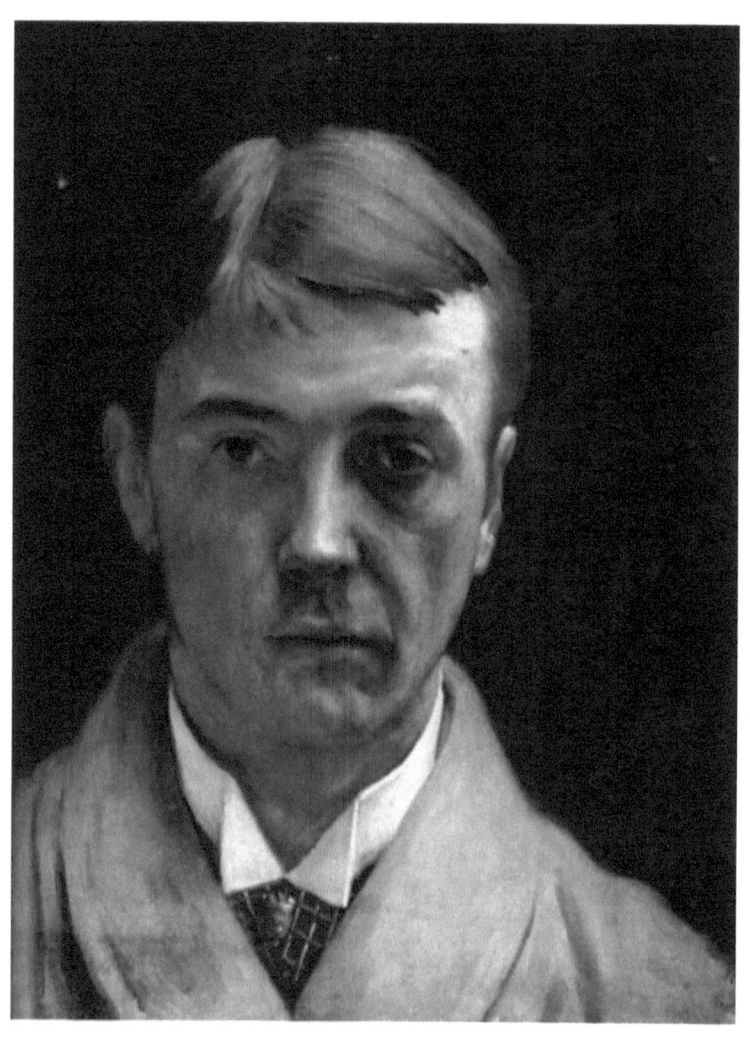

My portrait, 1891, oil on canvas

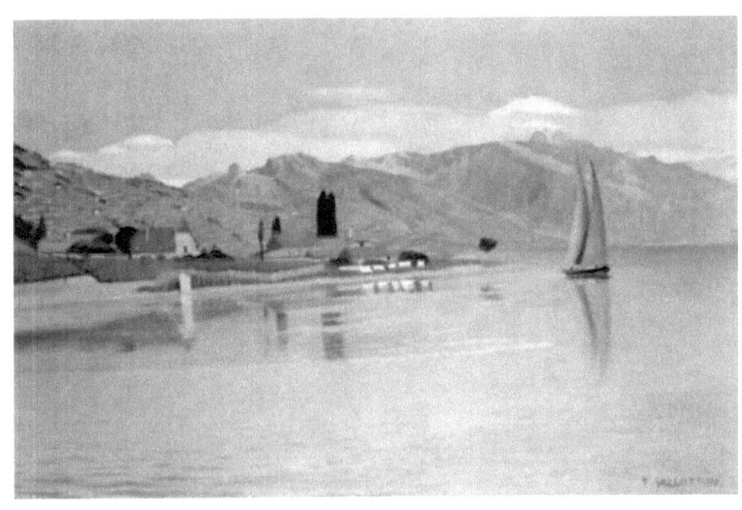

The Port of Pully, 1891, oil on canvas

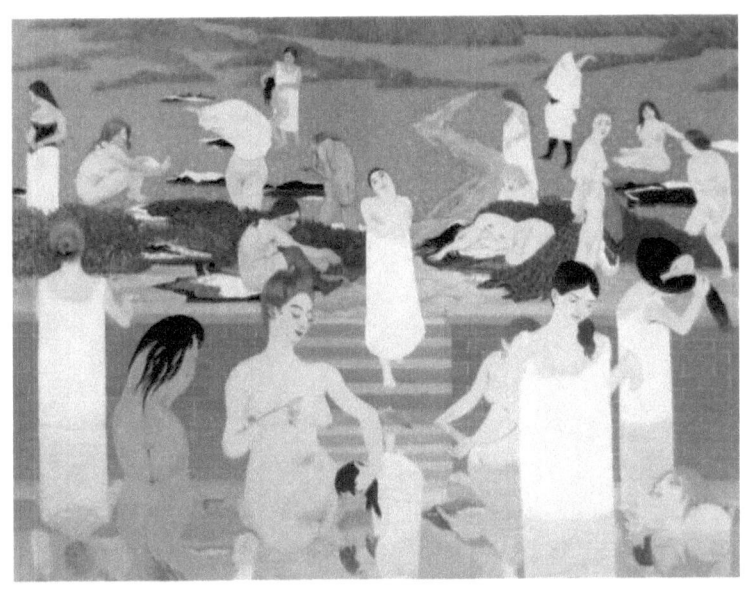

The Bath, Summer Evening, 1892, oil on canvas

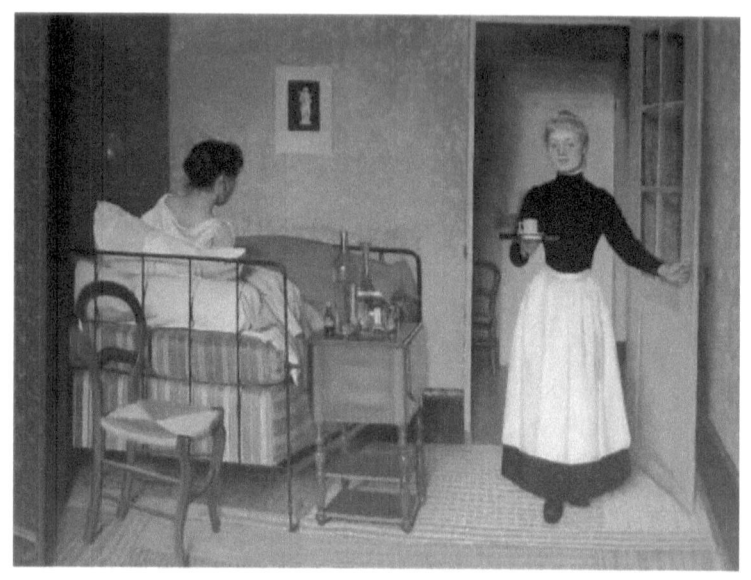

The Patient, 1892, oil on canvas

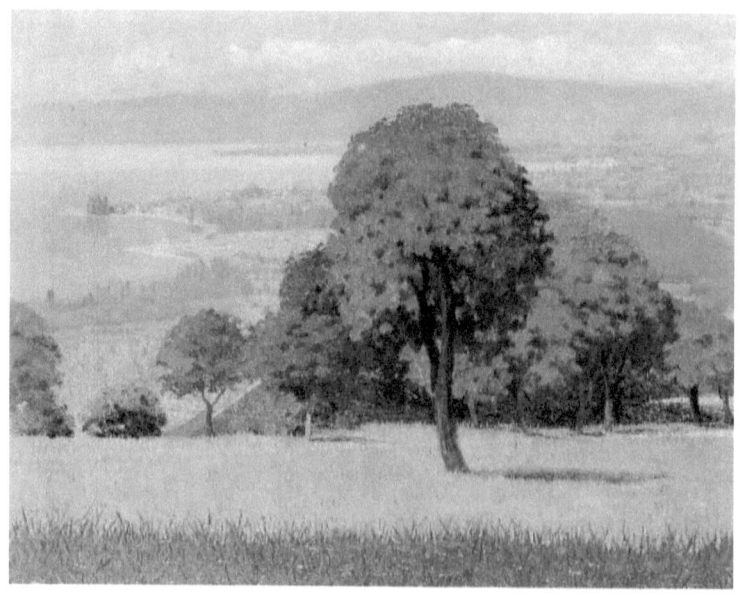

Outskirts of Lausanne, 1893, oil on canvas

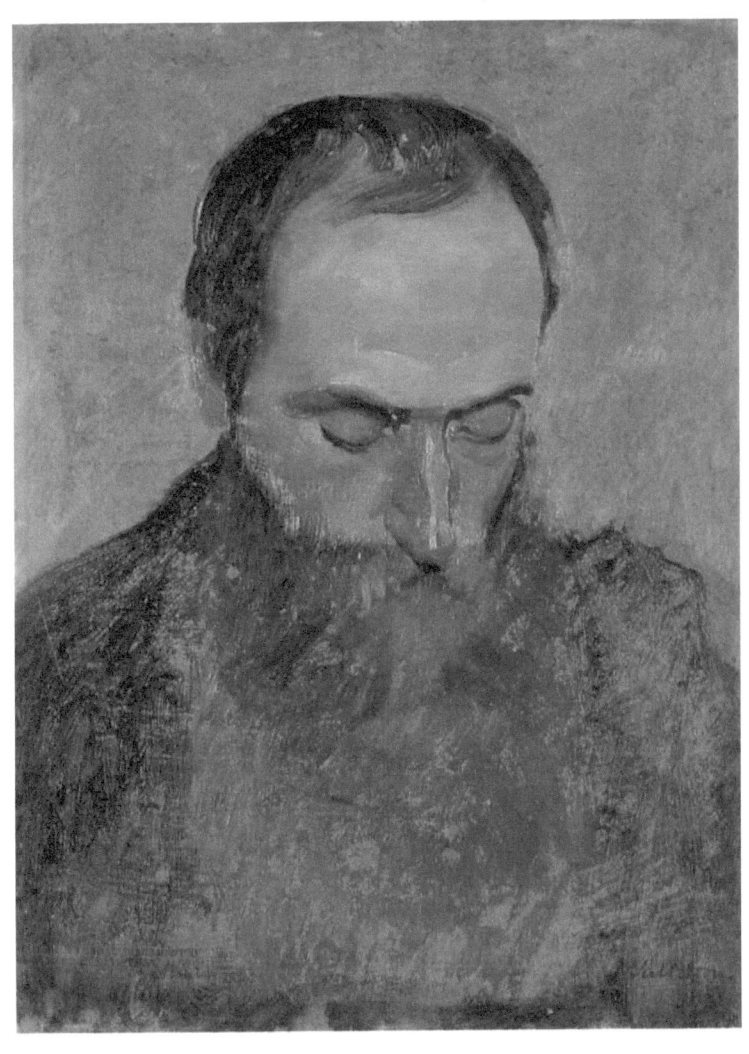

Portrait of Edouard Vuillard, 1893, oil on canvas

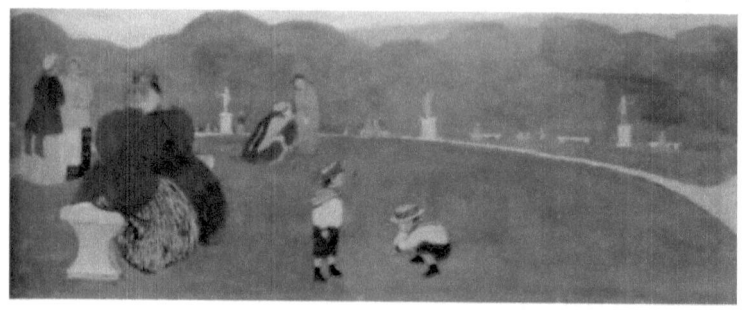

The Garden of Luxembourg, 1893, oil on canvas

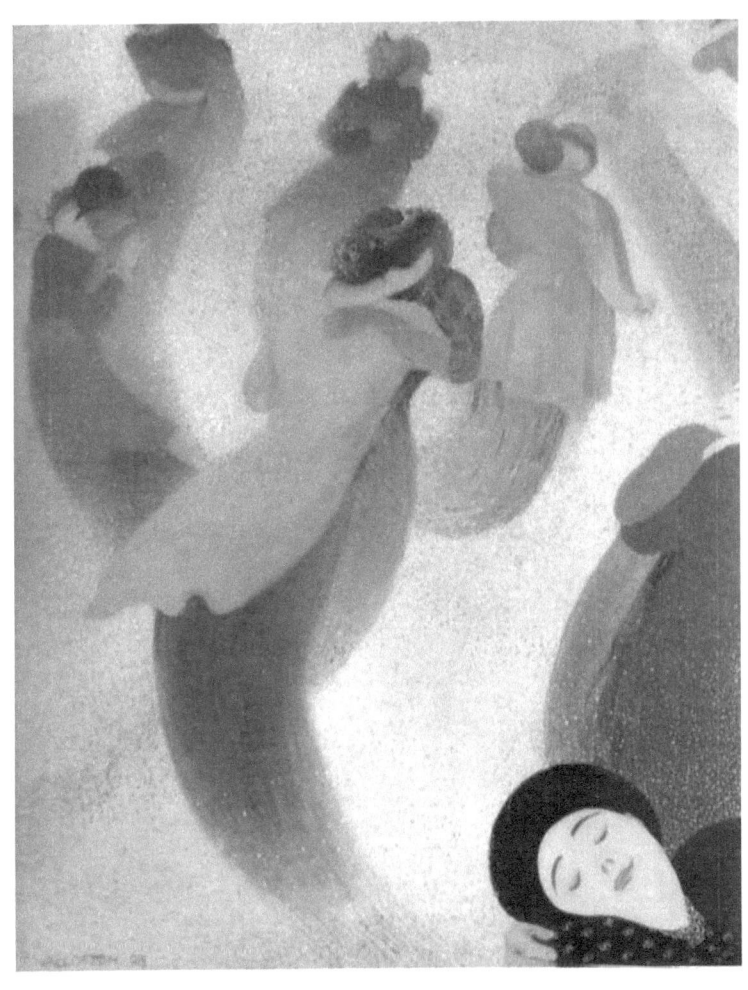

The Waltz, 1893, oil on canvas

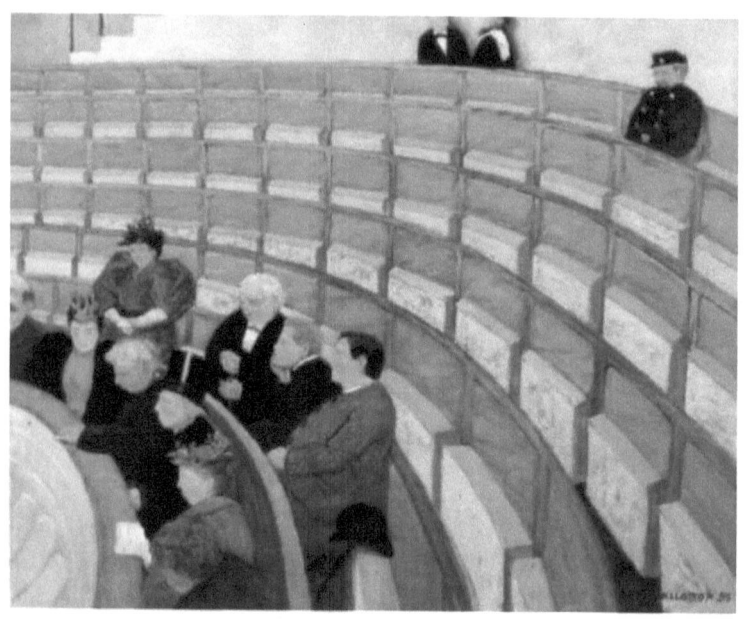

The Third Gallery at The Theatre, 1894, oil on canvas

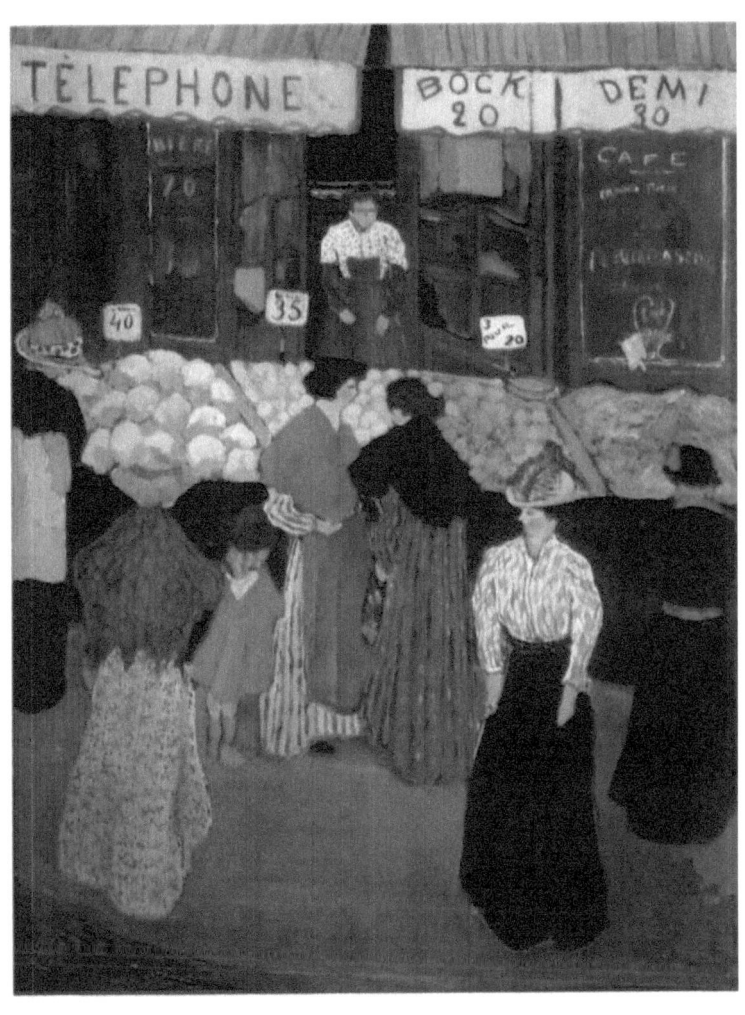

At the Market, 1895, oil on canvas

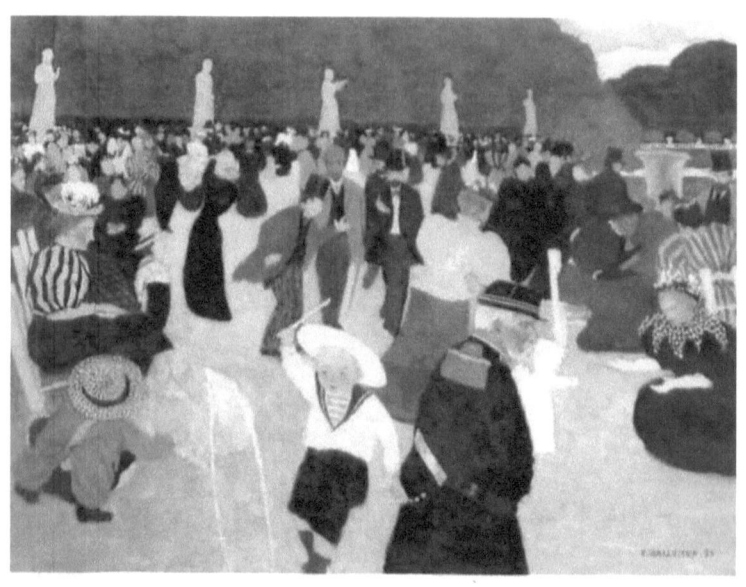

Luxembourg Garden, 1895, oil on canvas

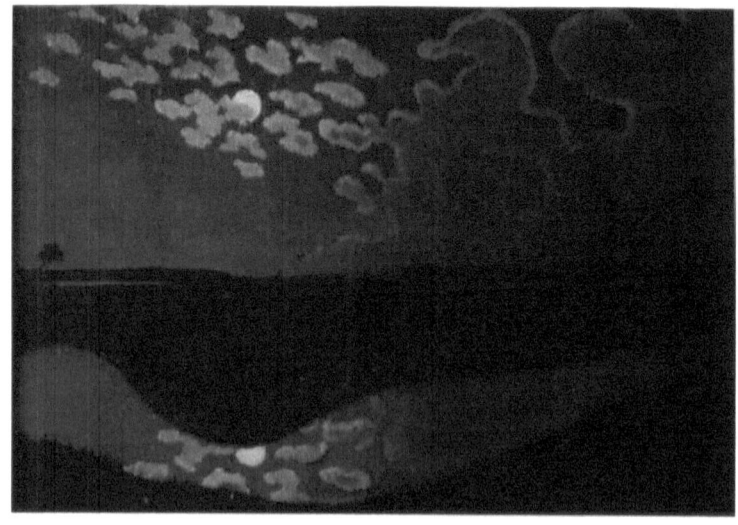

Moonlight, 1894-1895, oil on canvas

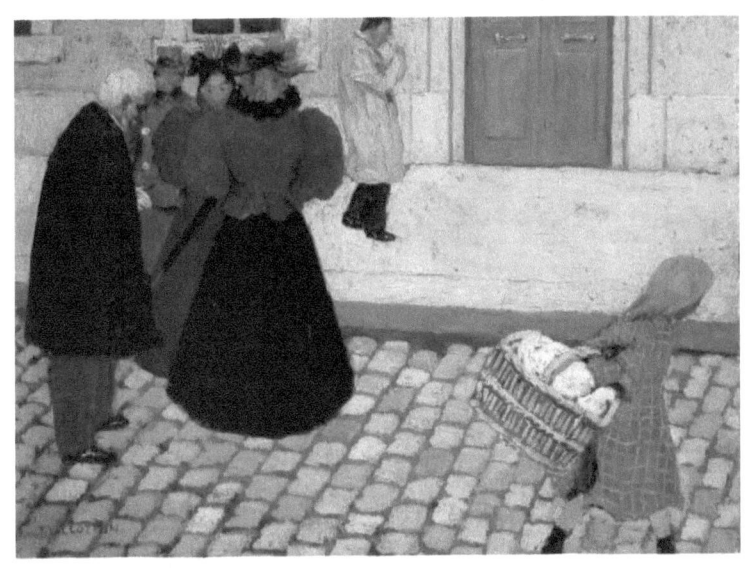

Street Scene, 1895, oil on canvas

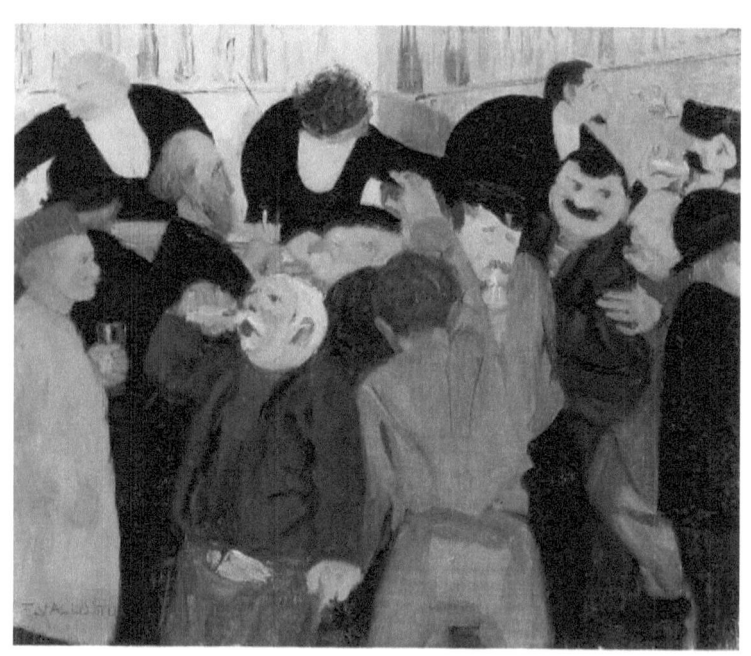

The Bistro, c.1895, oil on canvas

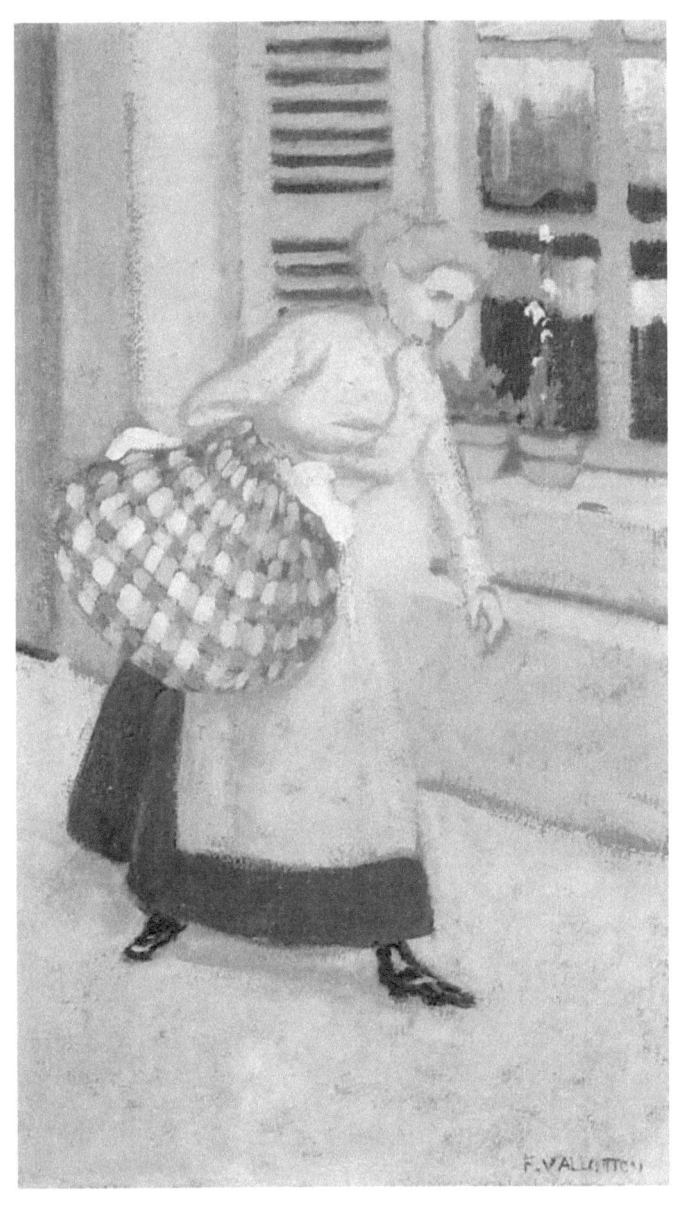

The Laundress, 1895, oil on canvas

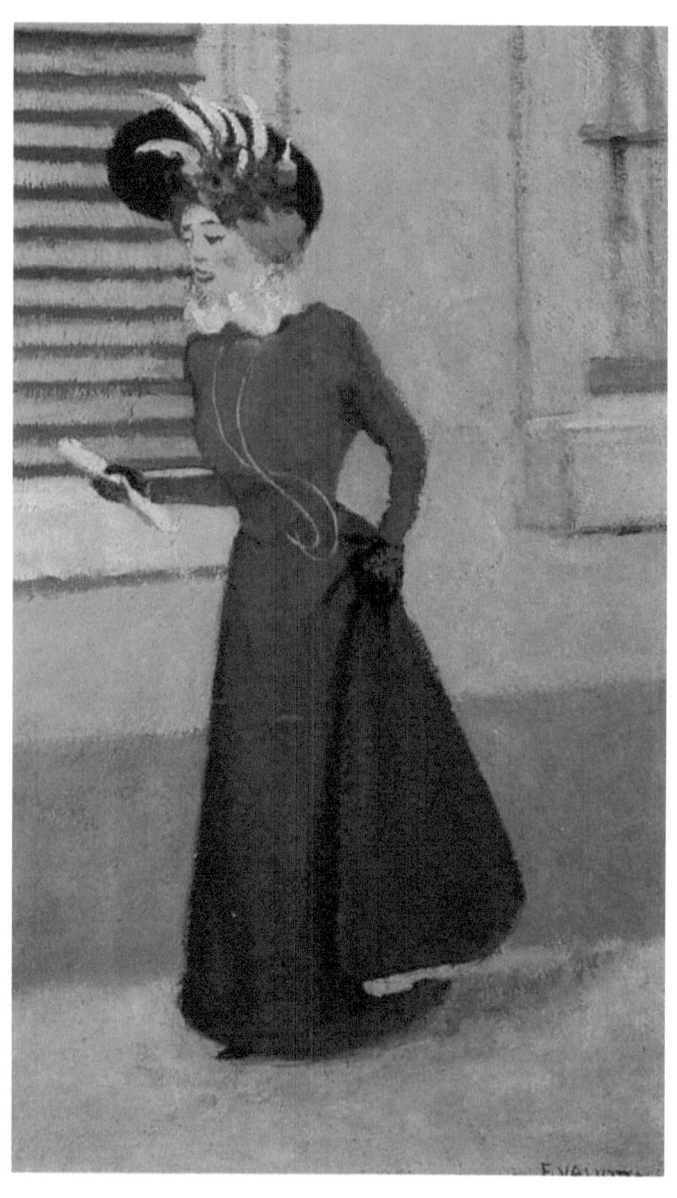

Woman with a Plumed Hat, 1895, oil on canvas

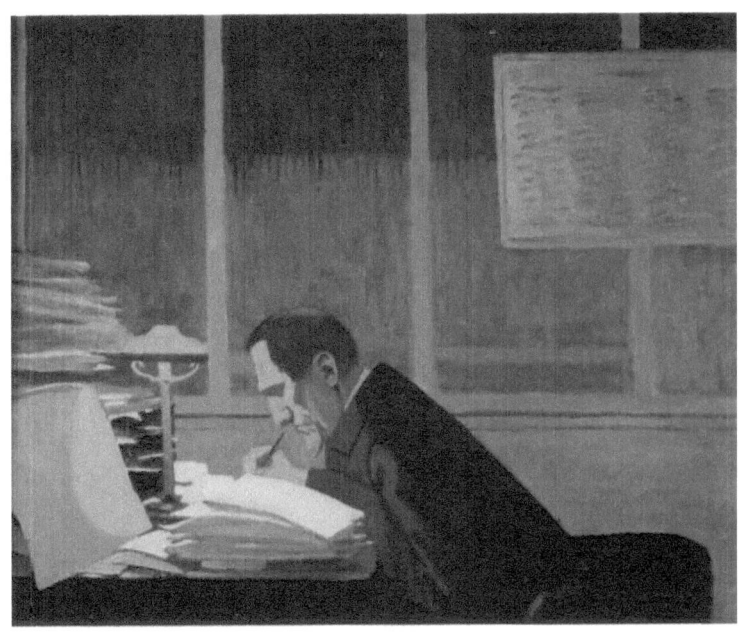

Felix Feneon at the Revue Blanche, 1896, oil on canvas

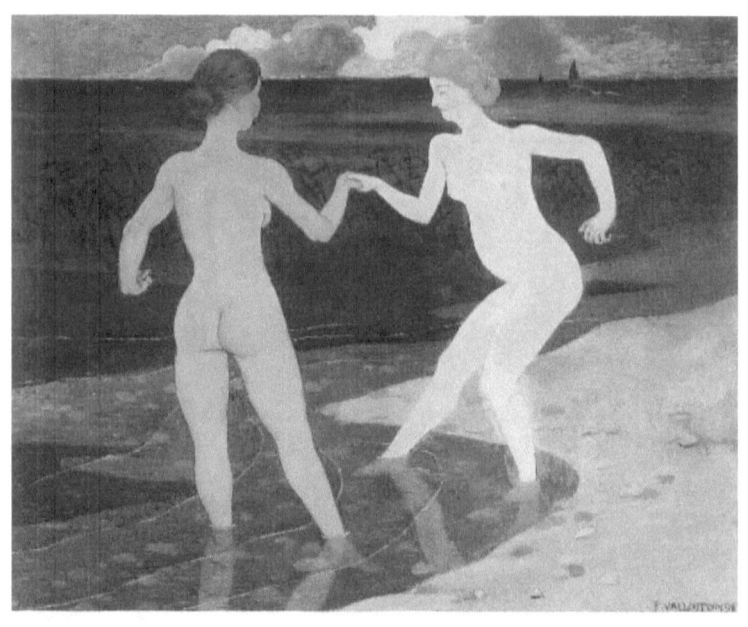

Woman with maid bathing, 1896, oil on canvas

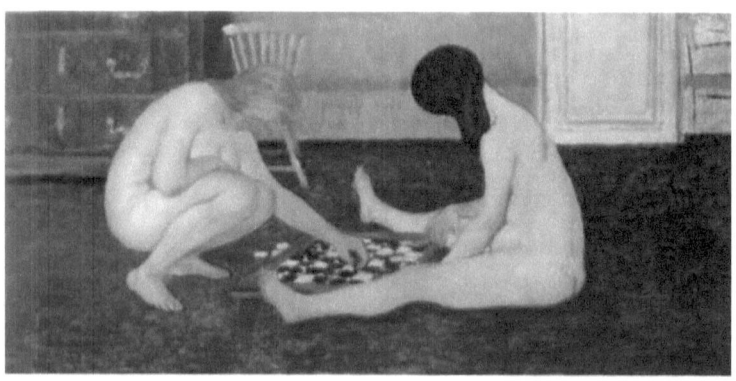

Naked Women Playing Checkers, 1897, oil on canvas

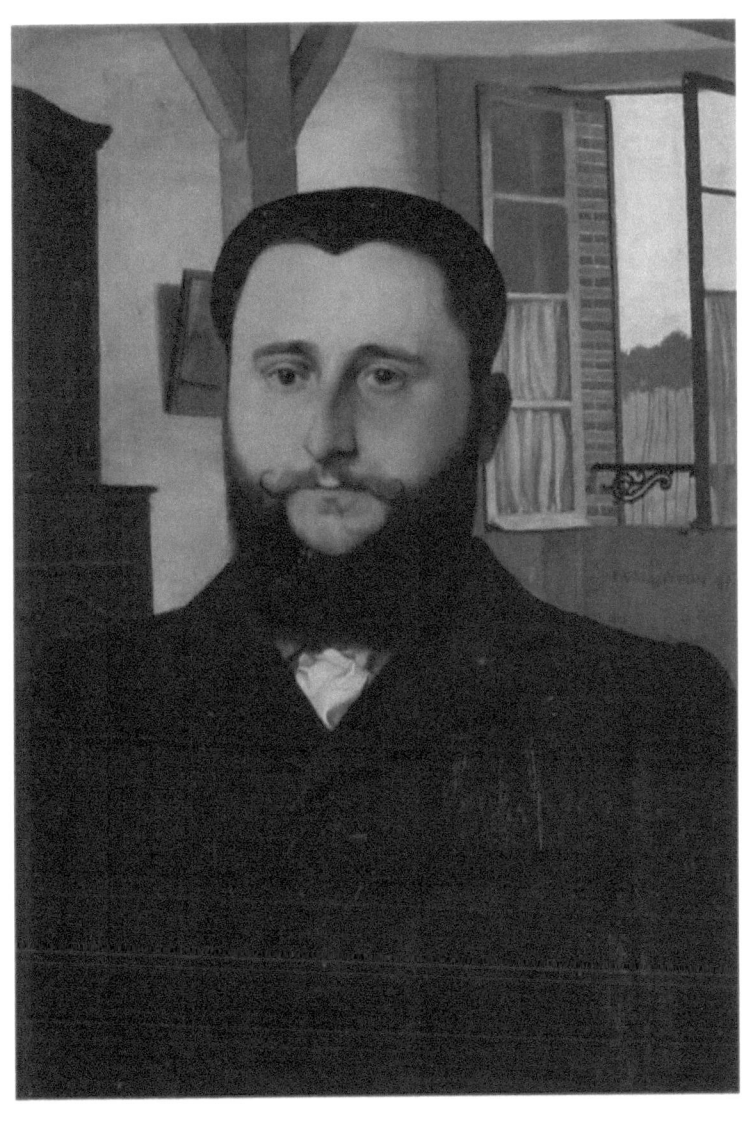

Portrait of Thadee Nathanson, 1897, oil on canvas

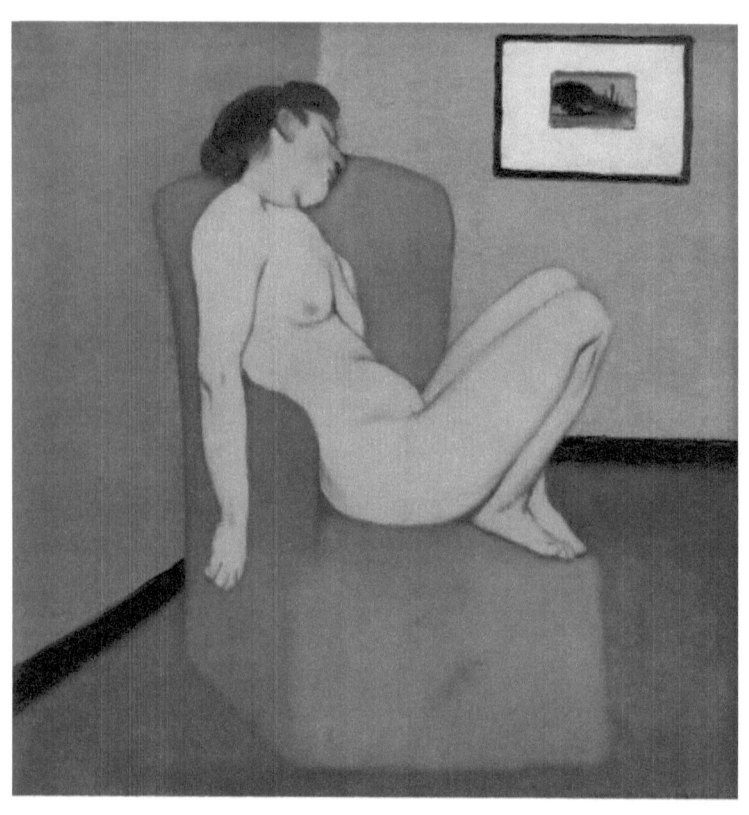

Seated Female Nude, 1897, oil on canvas

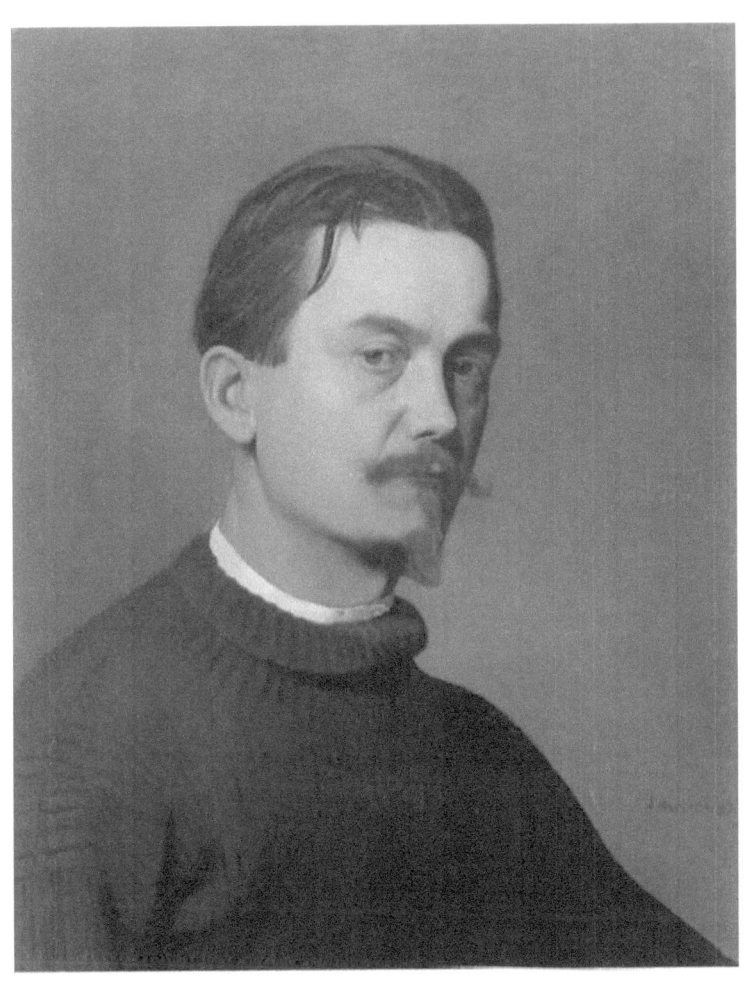

Self-portrait, 1897, oil on cart-board

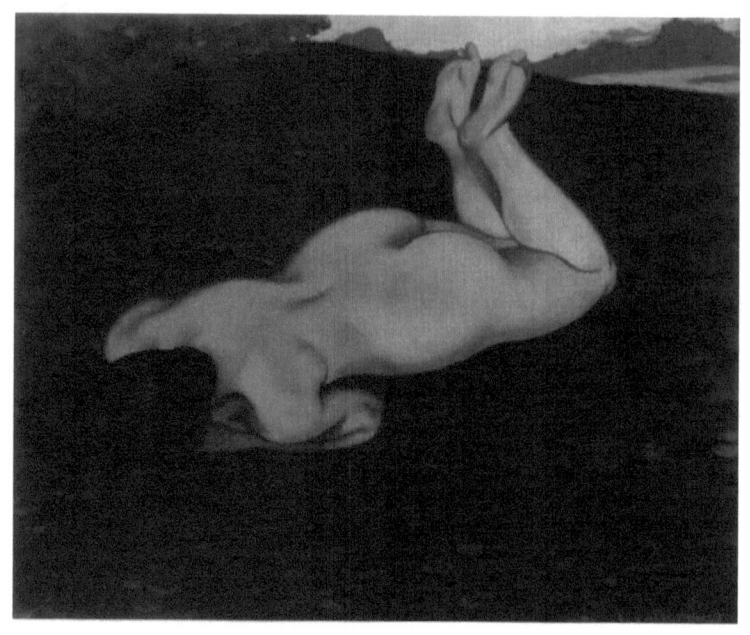

The Source, 1897, oil on canvas

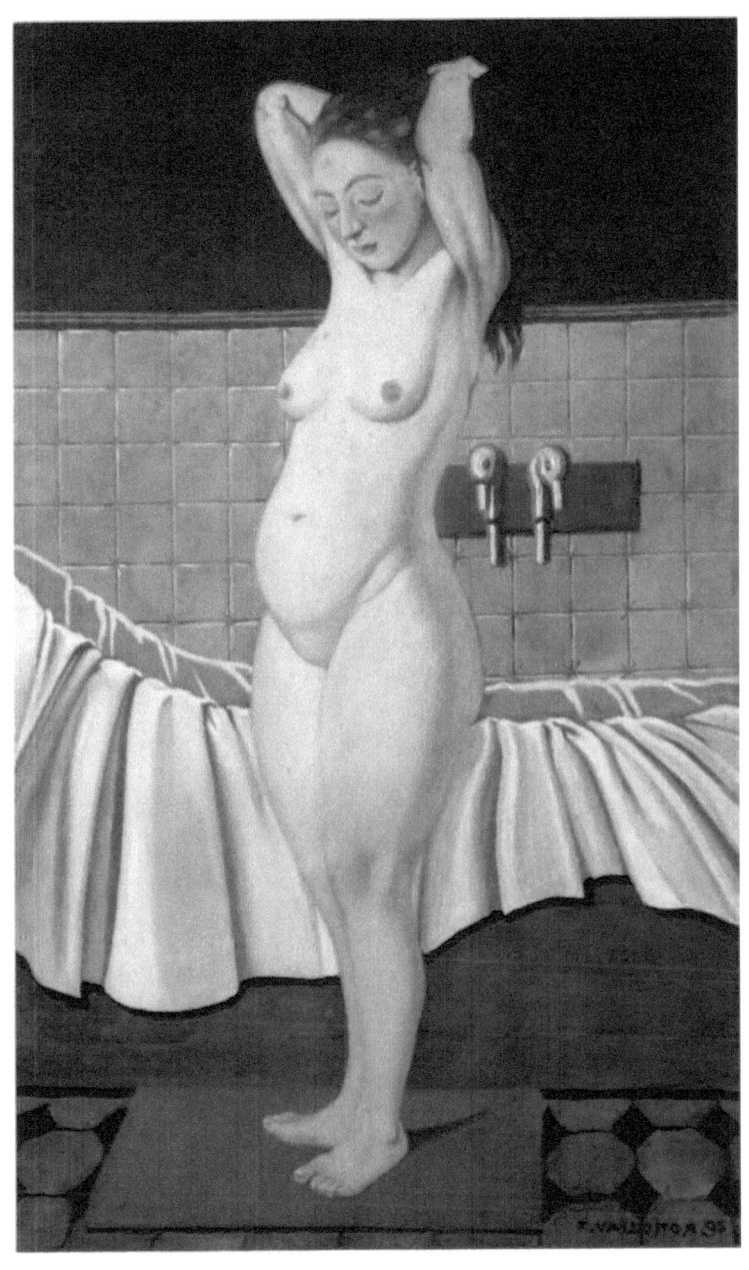

Woman in Bath, 1897, tempera

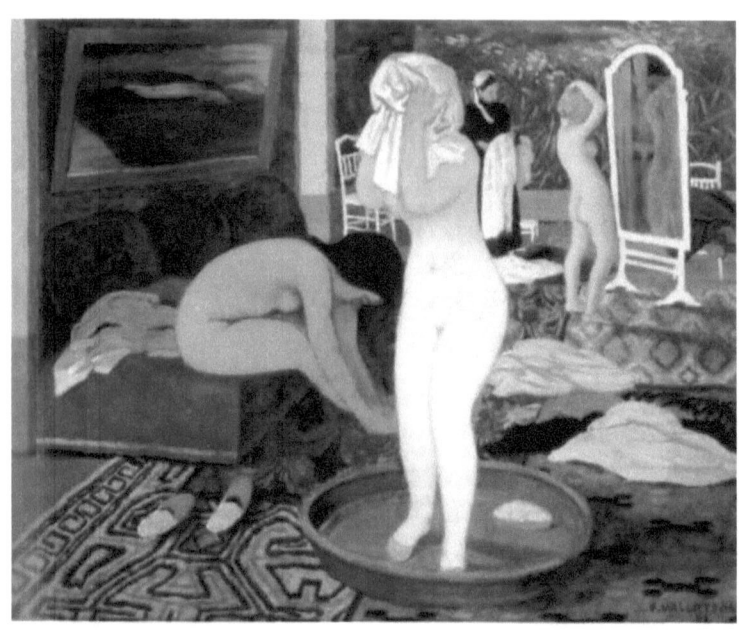

Women at Their Toilet, 1897, oil on cardboard

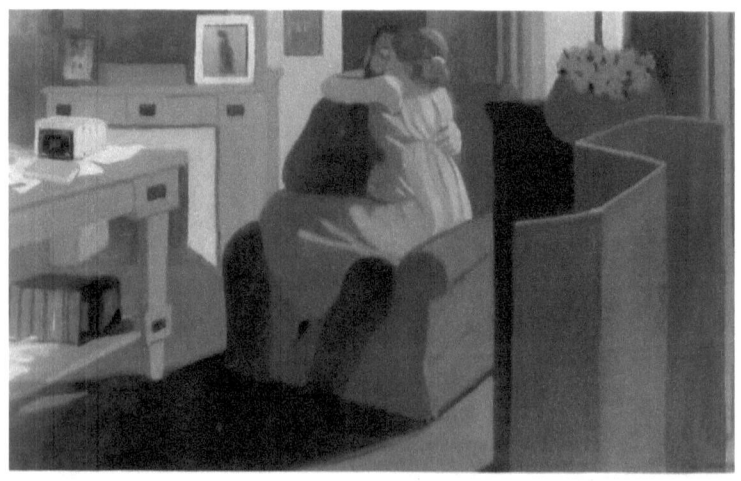

Intimacy Couple in Interior, 1898, oil on canvas

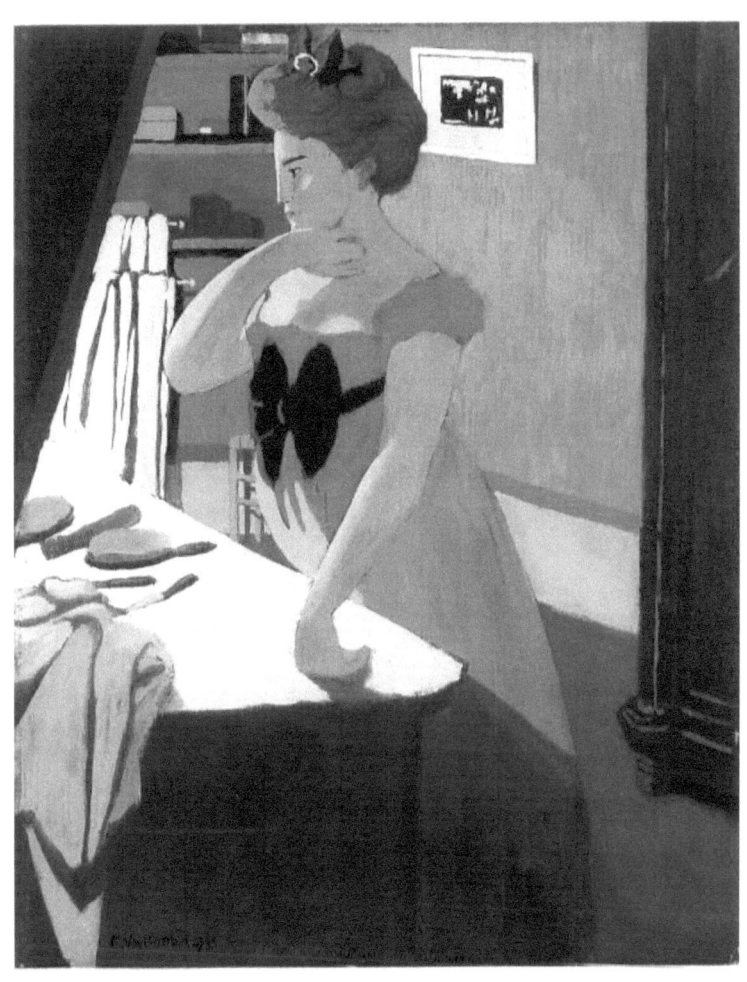

Misia at Her Dressing Table, 1898, tempera

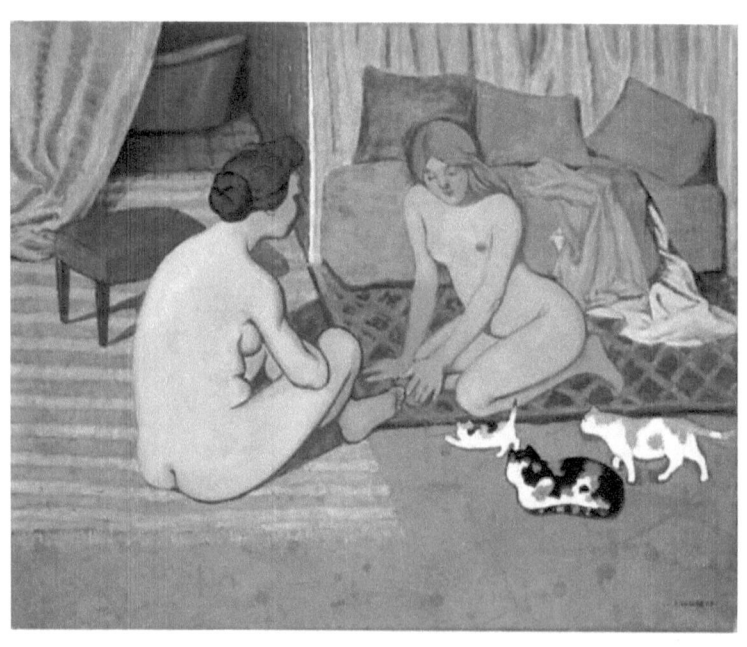

Naked women to cats, c.1897-1898, oil on canvas

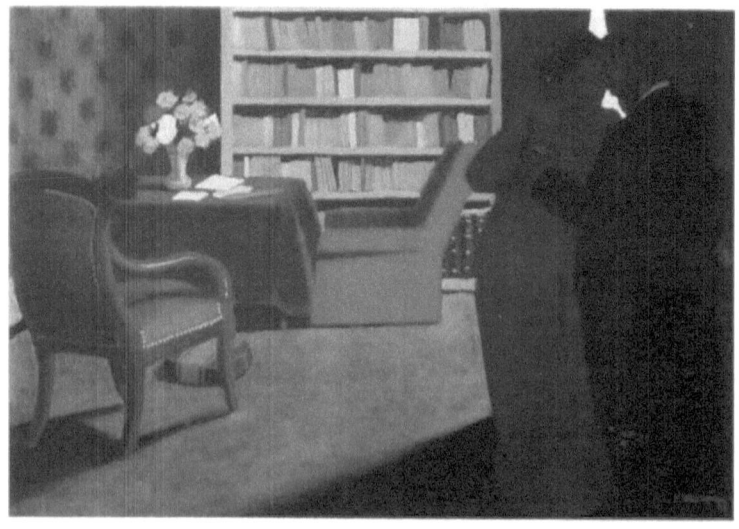

Private Conversation, 1898, oil on canvas

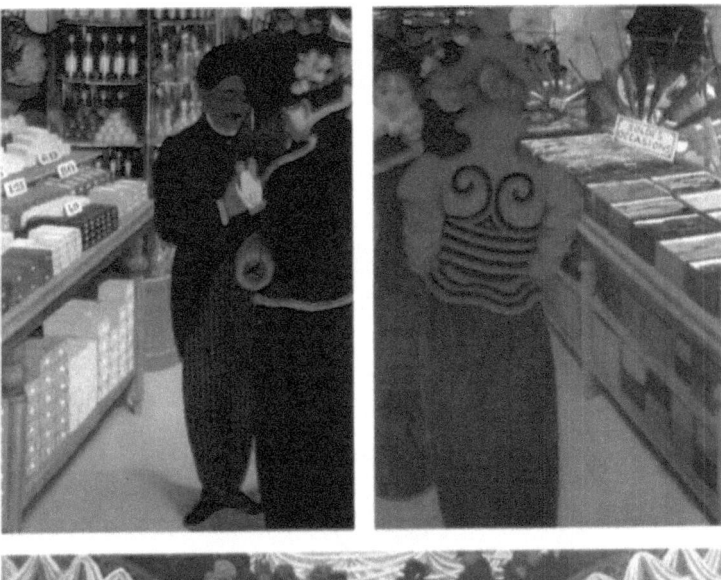

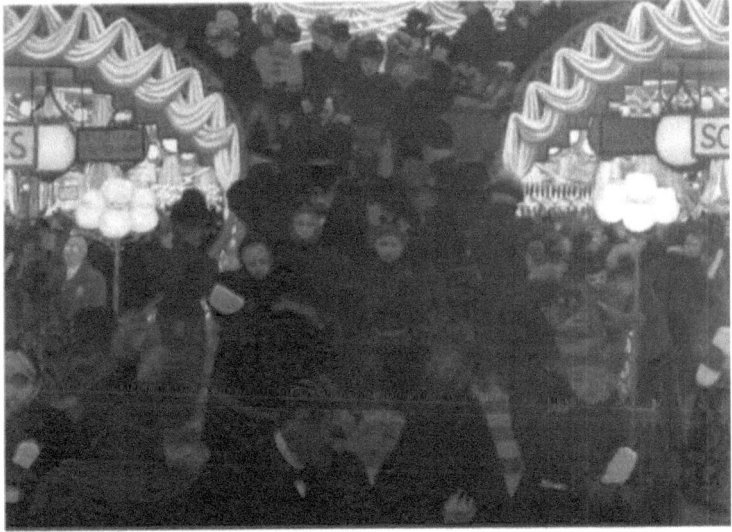

The Good market (Triptych), 1898, oil on canvas

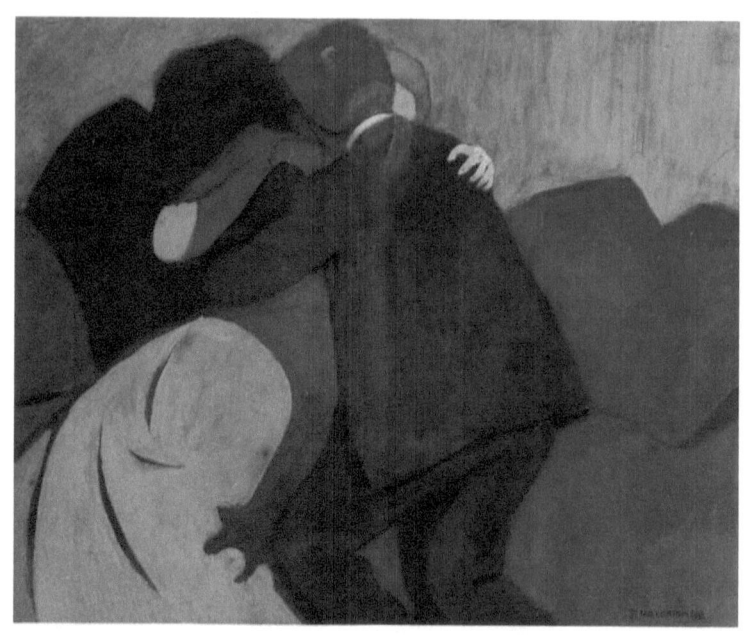

The Kiss, 1898, tempera

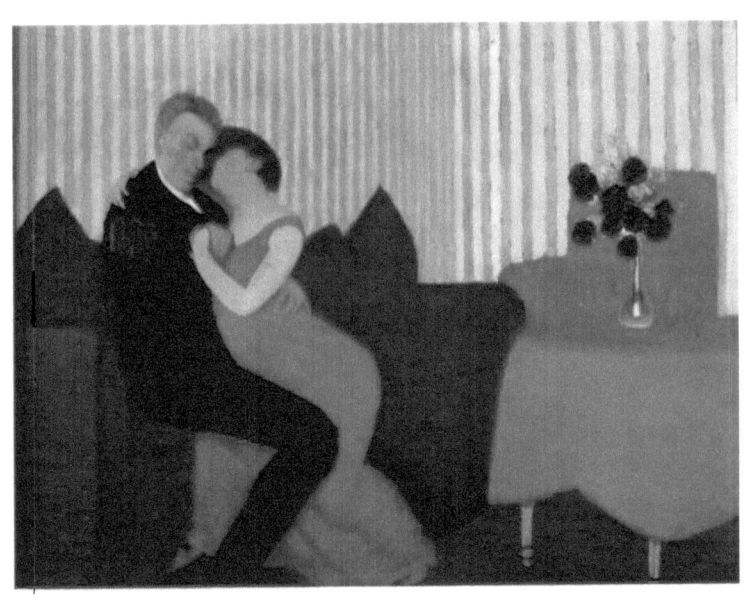

The Lie, 1898, oil on canvas

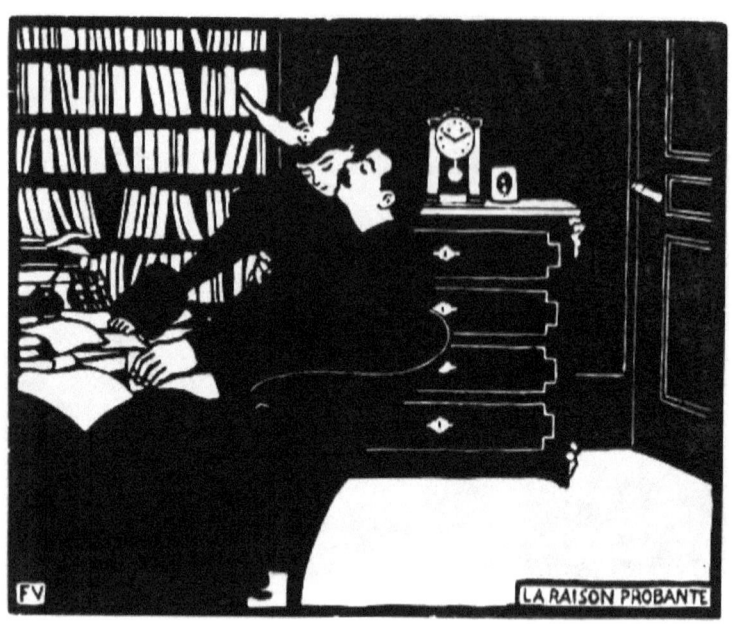

The compelling reason, 1898, woodcut

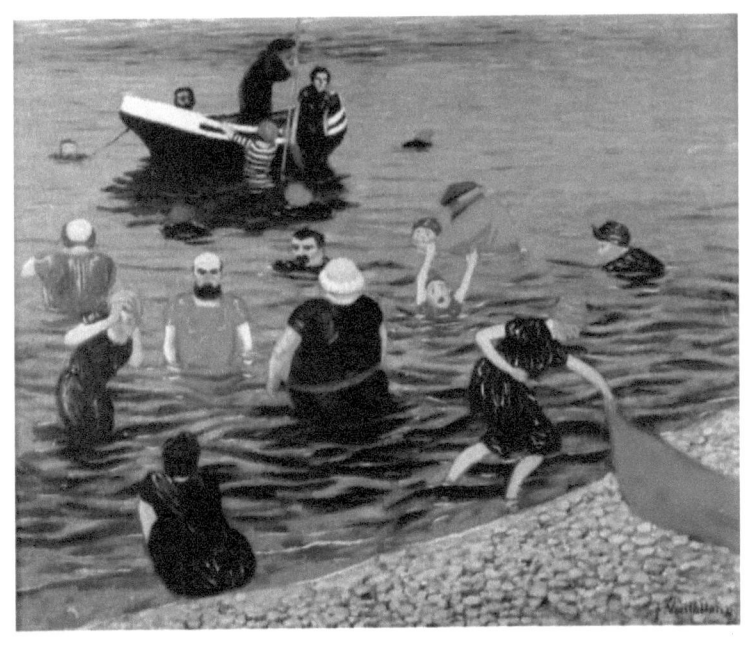

Bathing in Etretat, 1899, oil on canvas

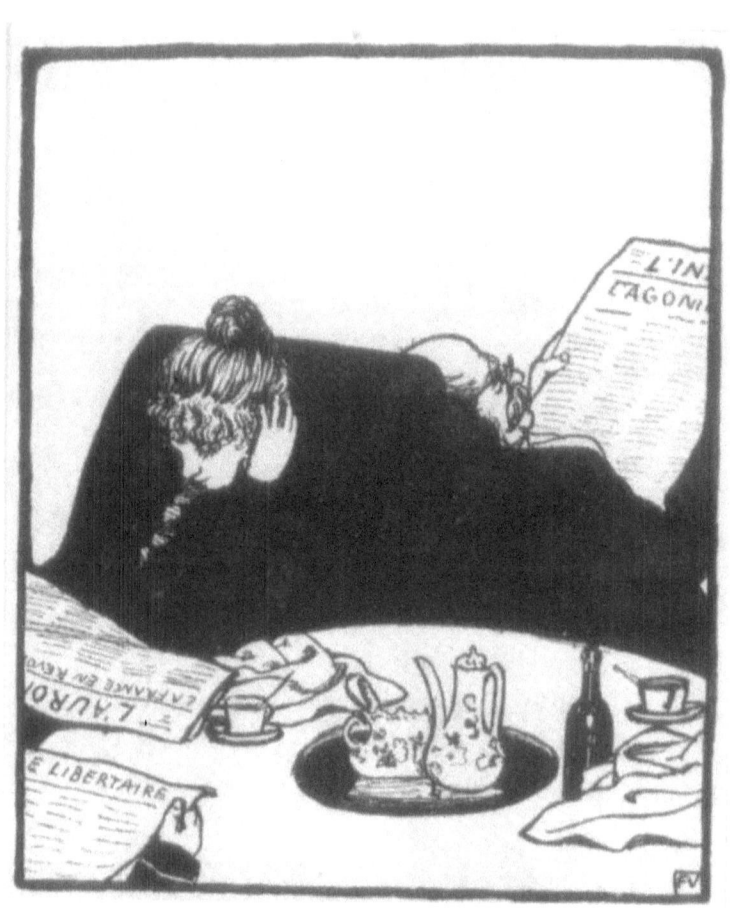

Family, 1899, woodcut

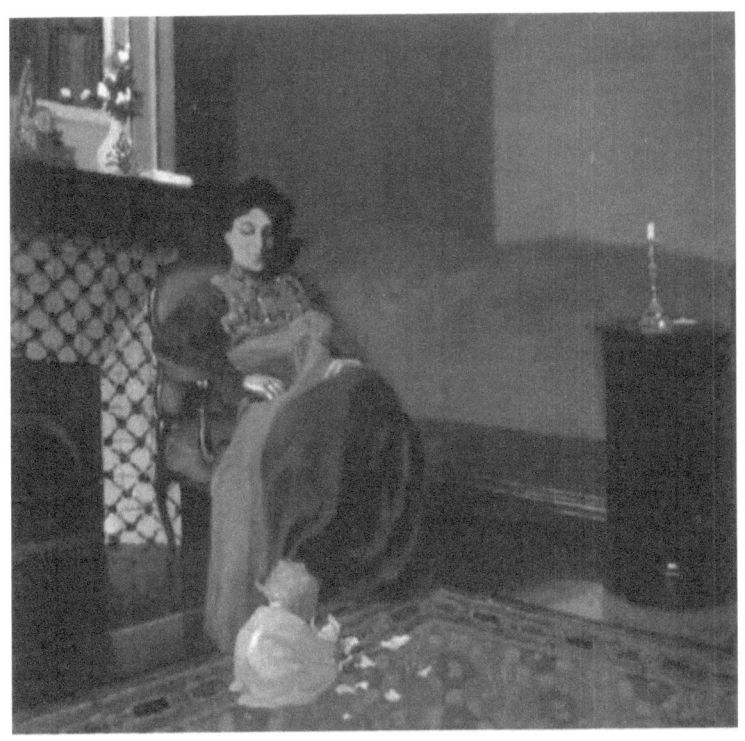

Interior Red Room with Woman and Child, 1899, oil on
canvas

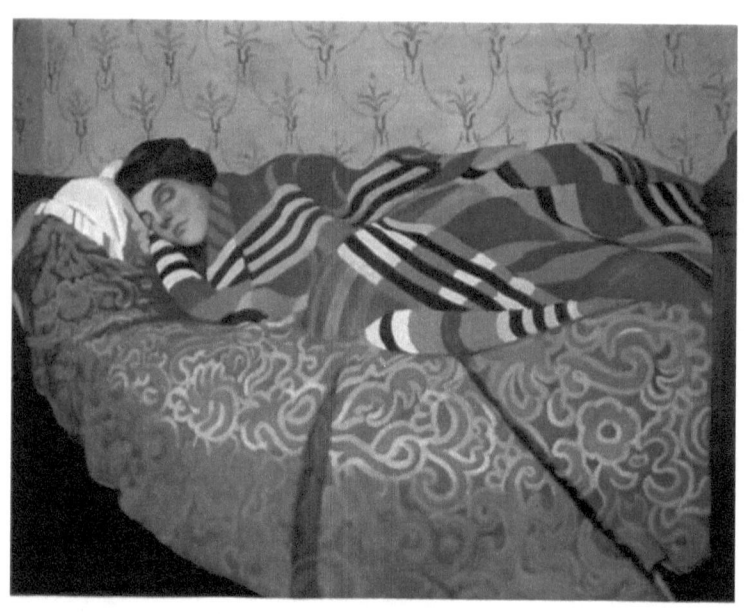

Laid down woman, sleeping, 1899, oil on canvas

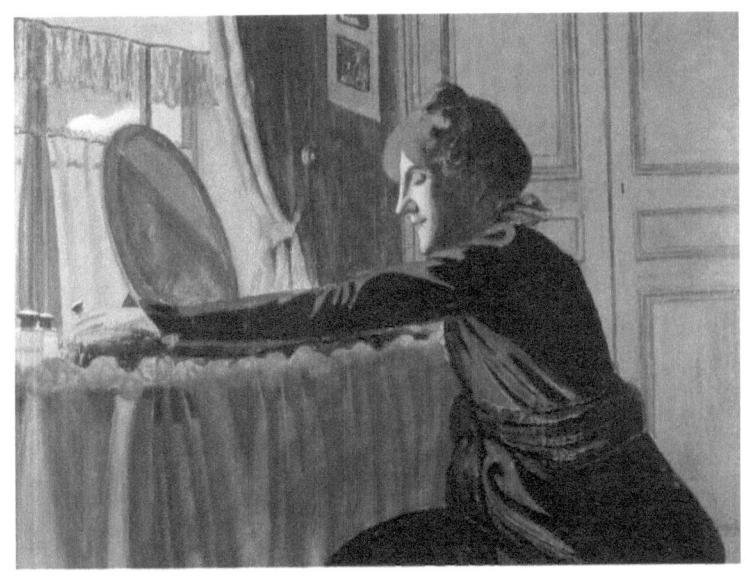

Madame Felix Vallotton at Her Dressing Table, 1899, oil on canvas

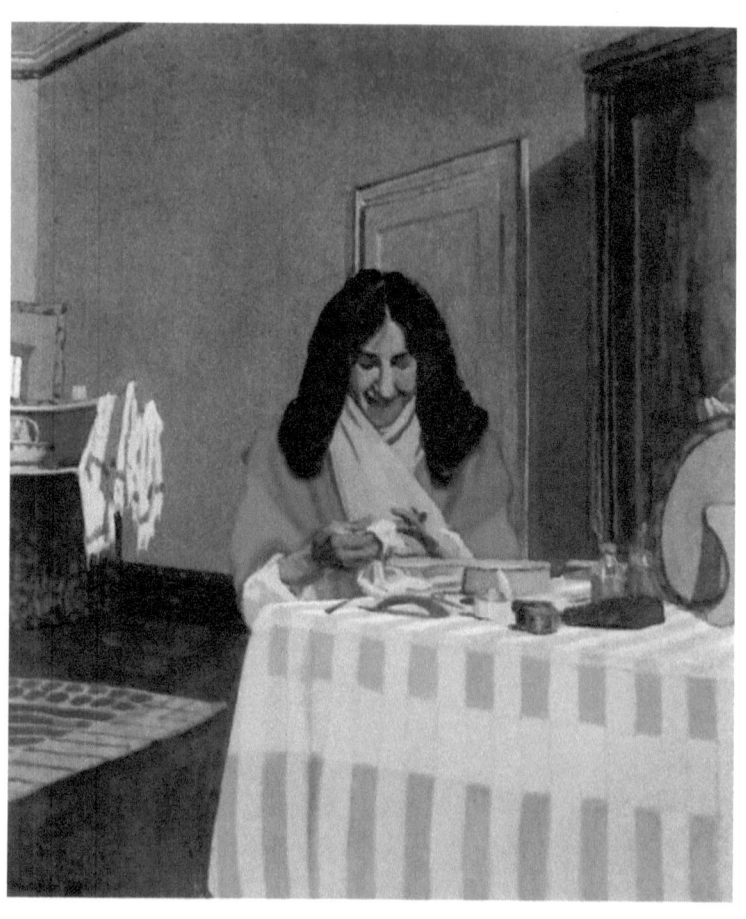

Mme. Felix Vallotton, 1899, oil on canvas

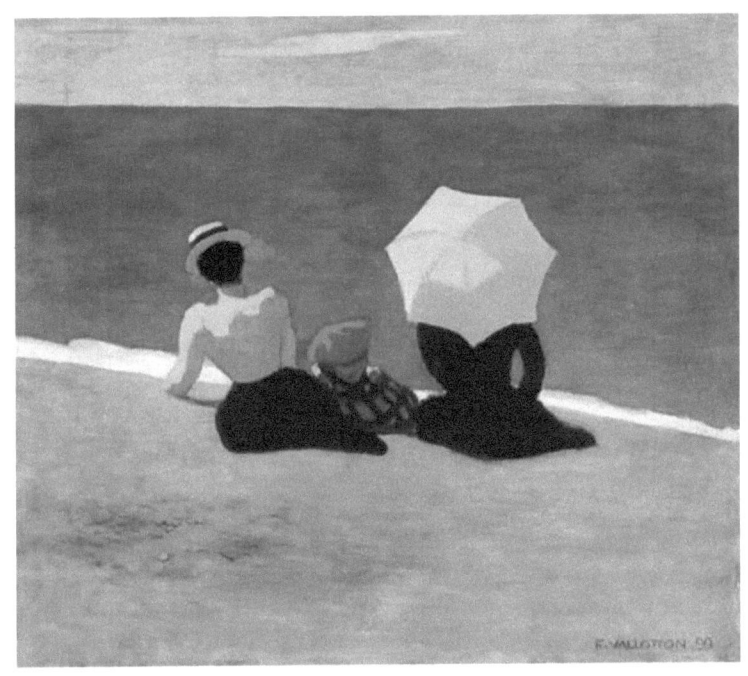

On the Beach, 1899, oil on canvas

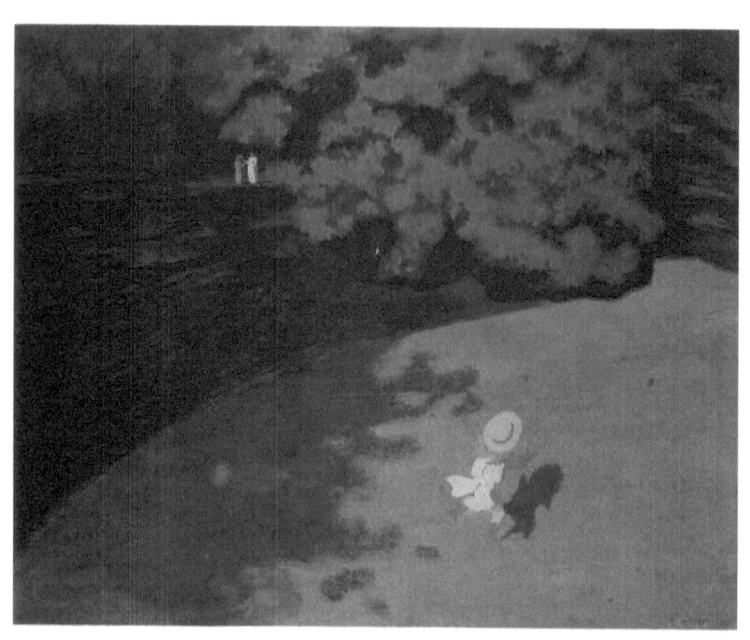

The Ball, 1899, oil on canvas

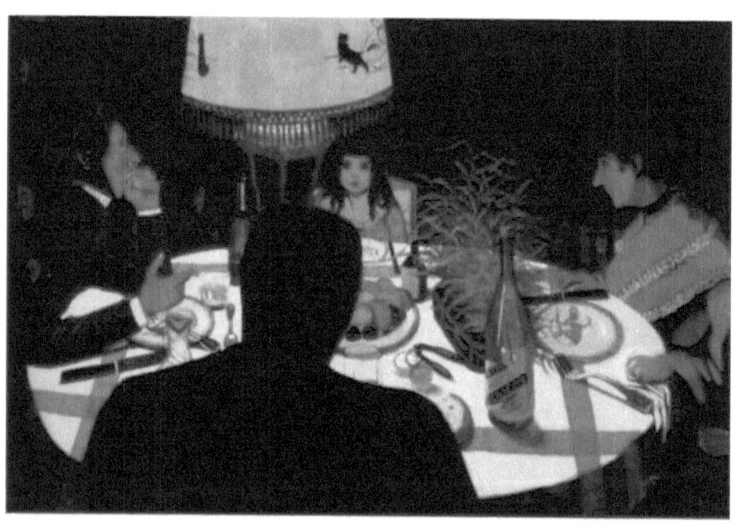

The Dinner, effect of lamp, 1899, oil on canvas

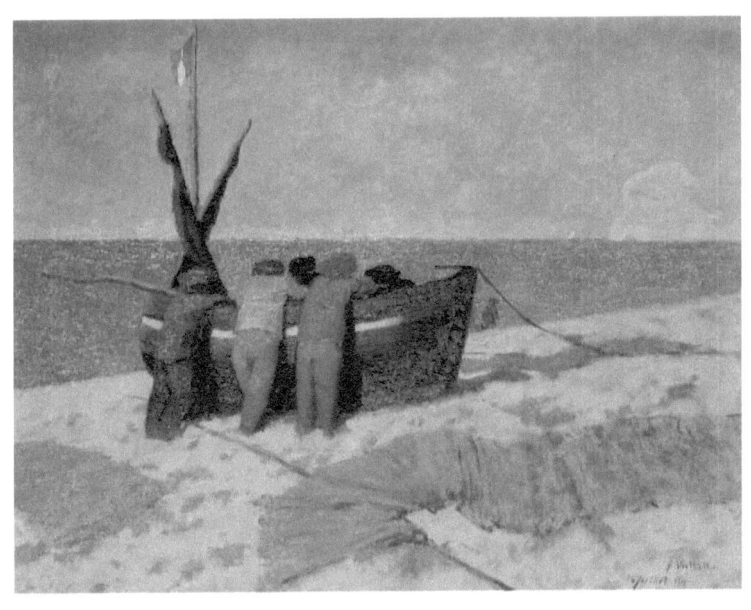

The Fourteenth of July at Etretat, 1899, oil on canvas

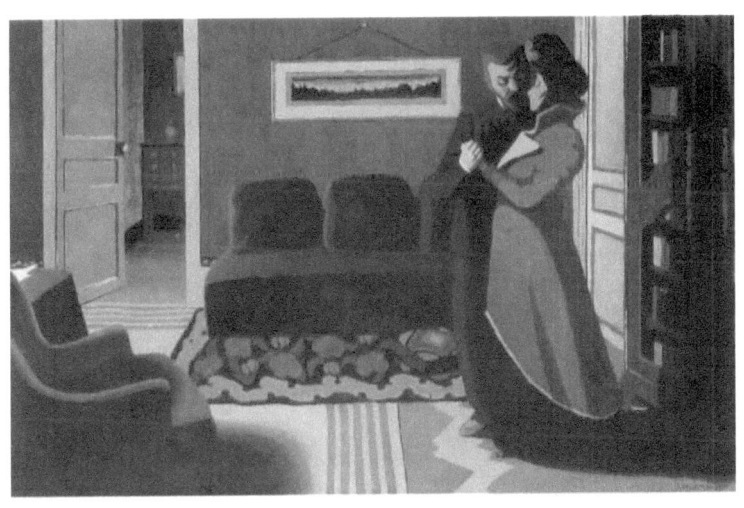

The Visit, 1899, tempera

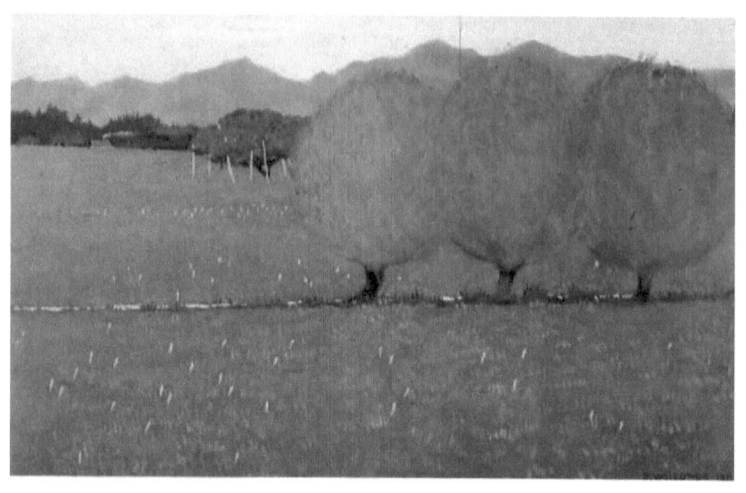

Autumn Crocuses, 1900, oil on canvas

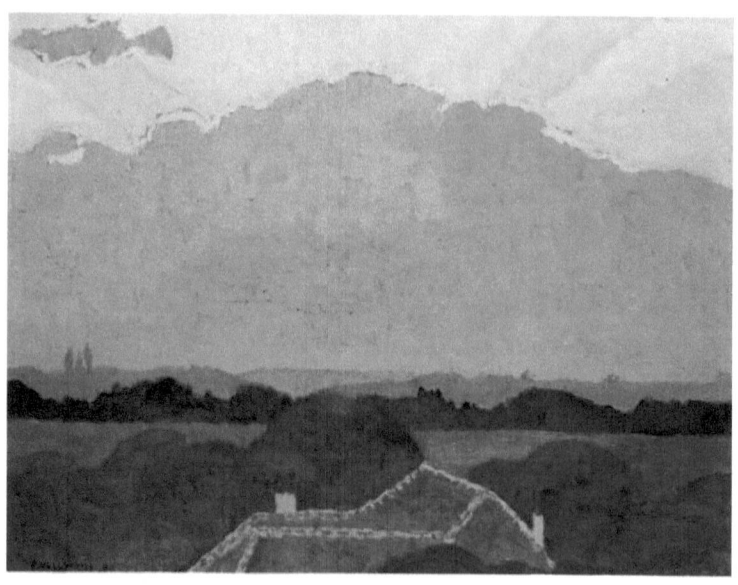

Cloud at Romanel, 1900, oil on canvas

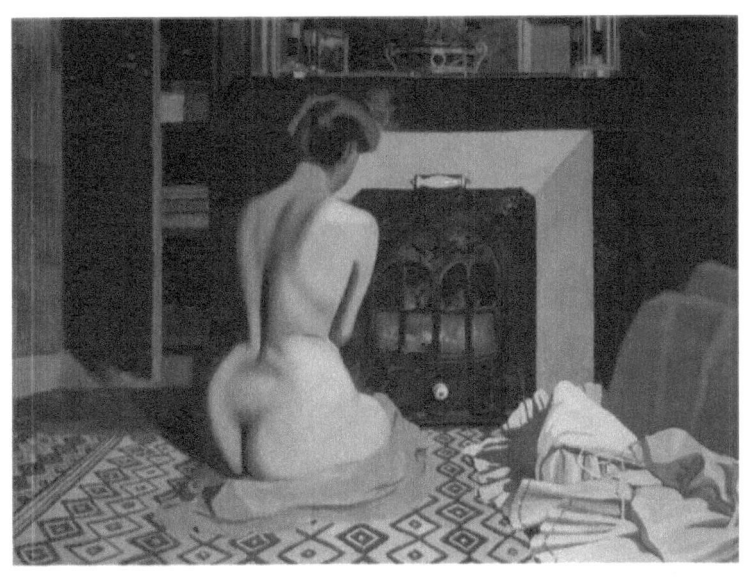

Nude at the Stove, 1900, oil on canvas

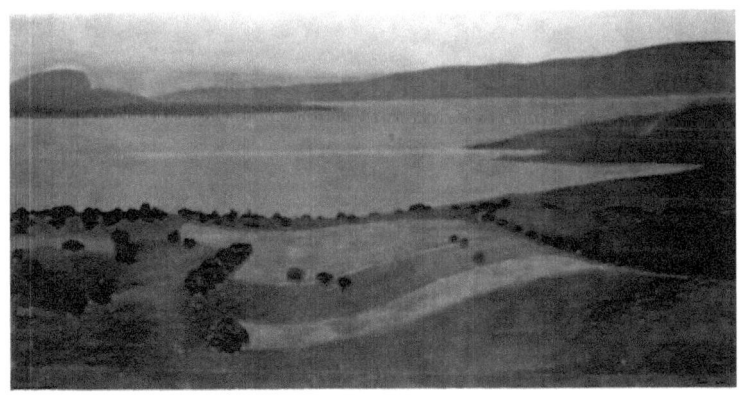

The Lake Leman, effect of the evening, 1900, tempera

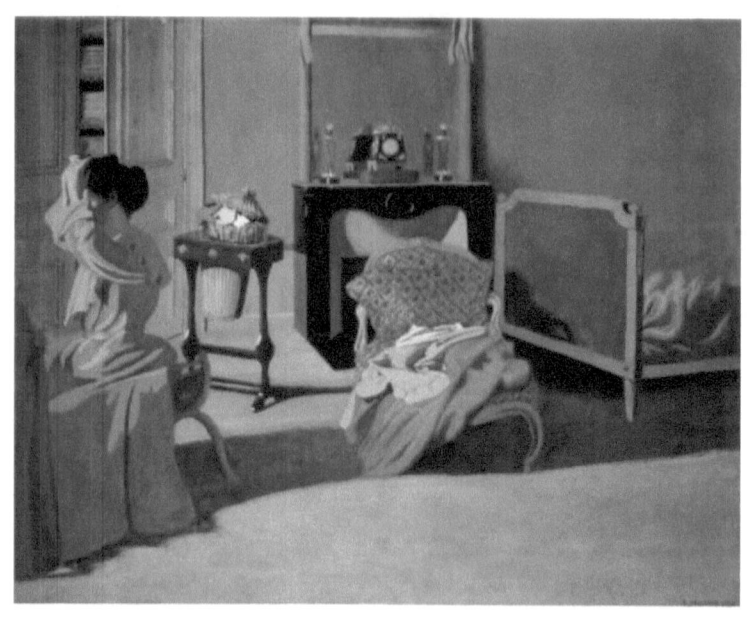

Woman being capped, 1900, oil on canvas

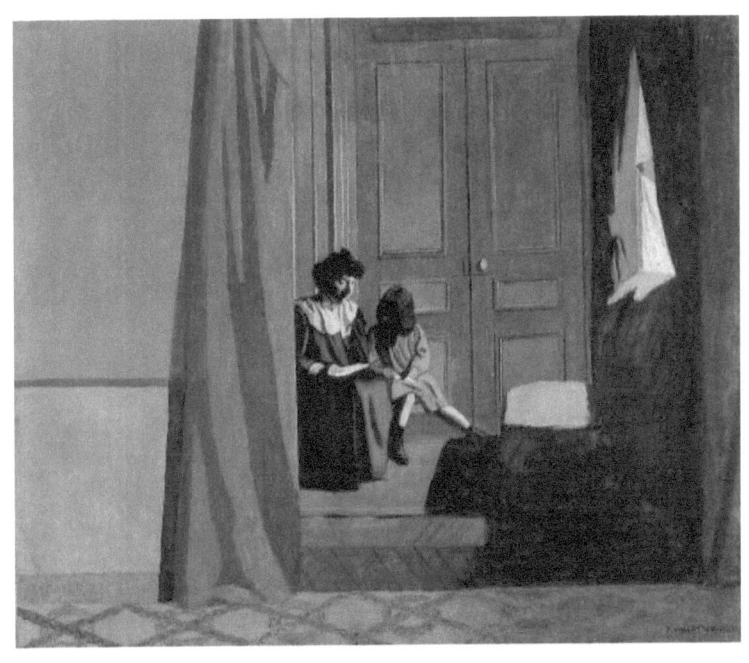

Woman Reading to a Little Girl, 1900, oil on canvas

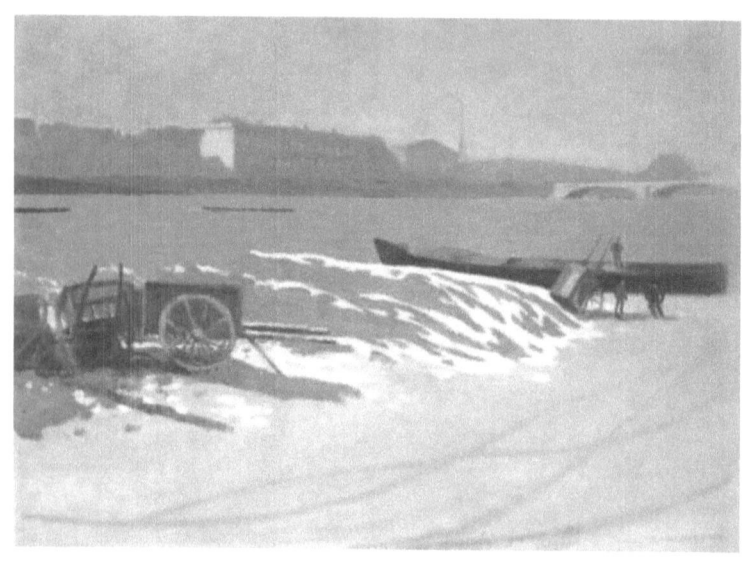

Red Sand and Snow, 1901, oil on canvas

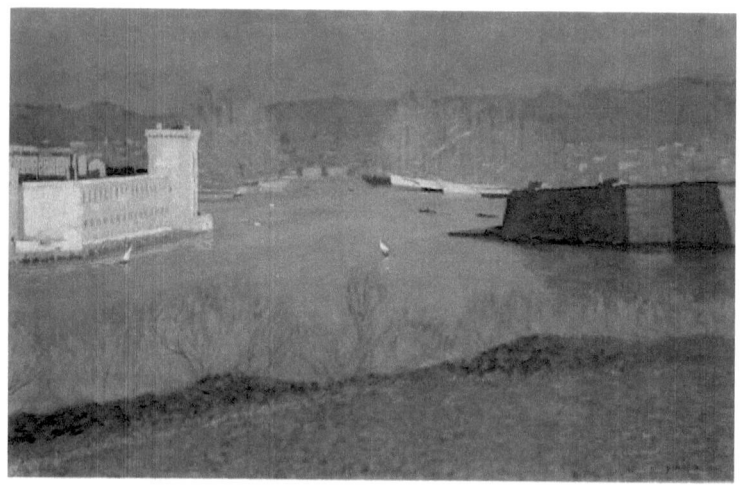

The Port of Marseille, 1901, oil on canvas

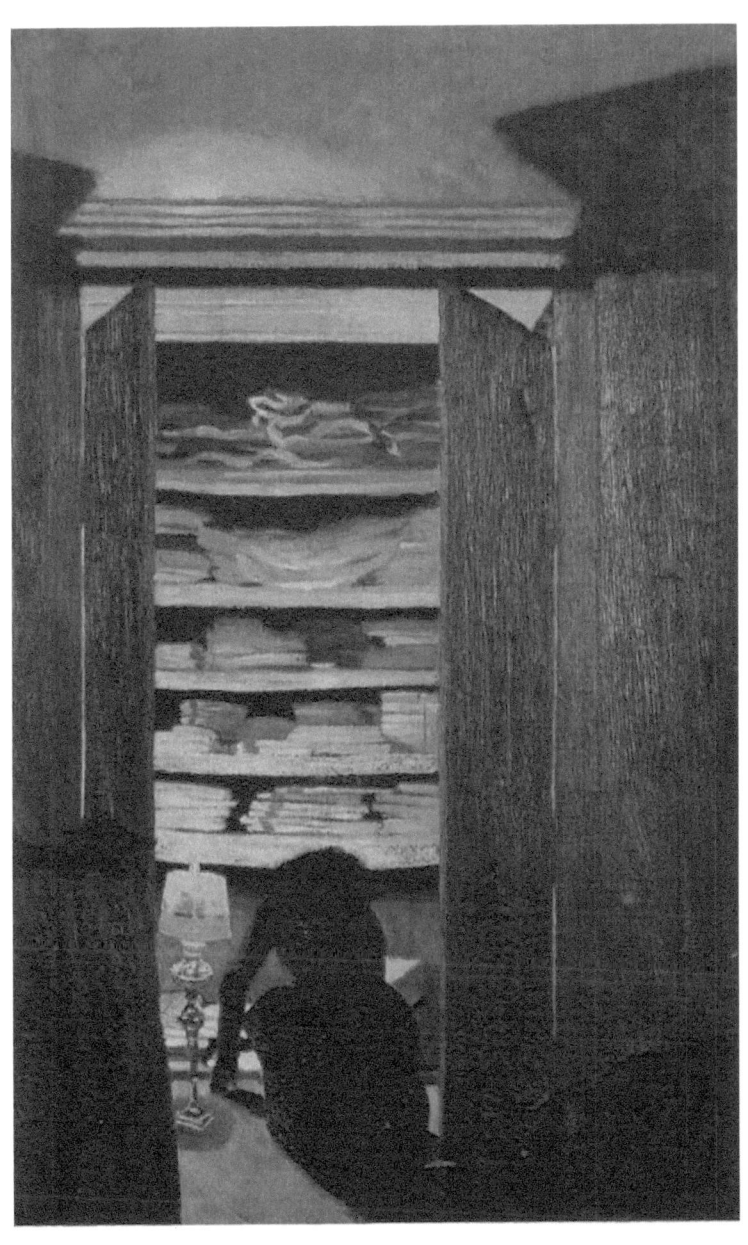

Woman searching through a Cupboard, 1900-1901, oil

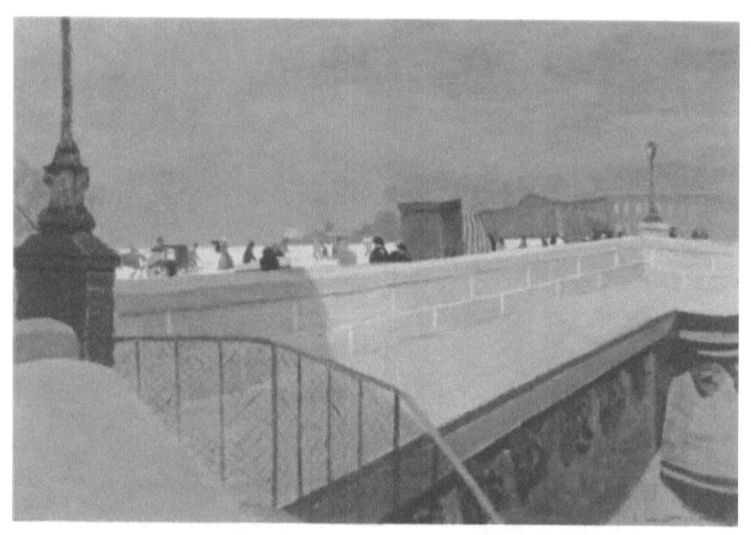

The Pont Neuf, 1901, oil

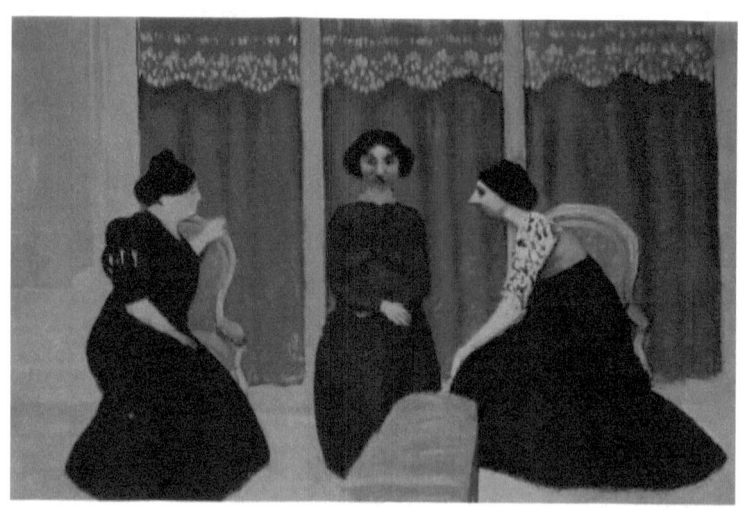

Gossip, 1902, oil on canvas

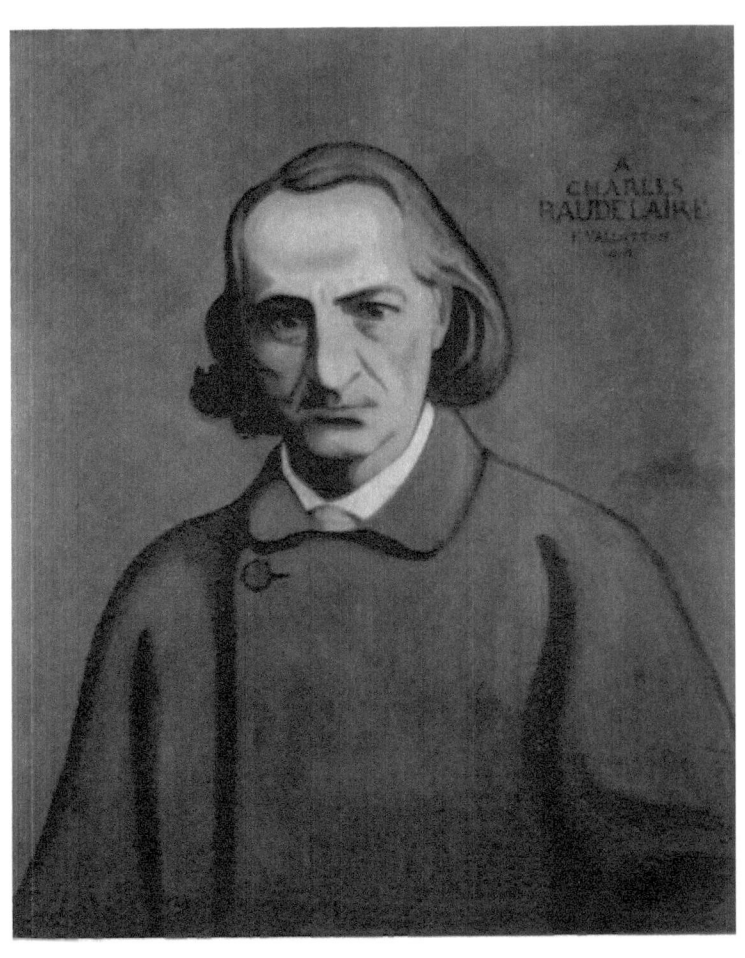

Portrait of Baudelaire, 1902, oil on canvas

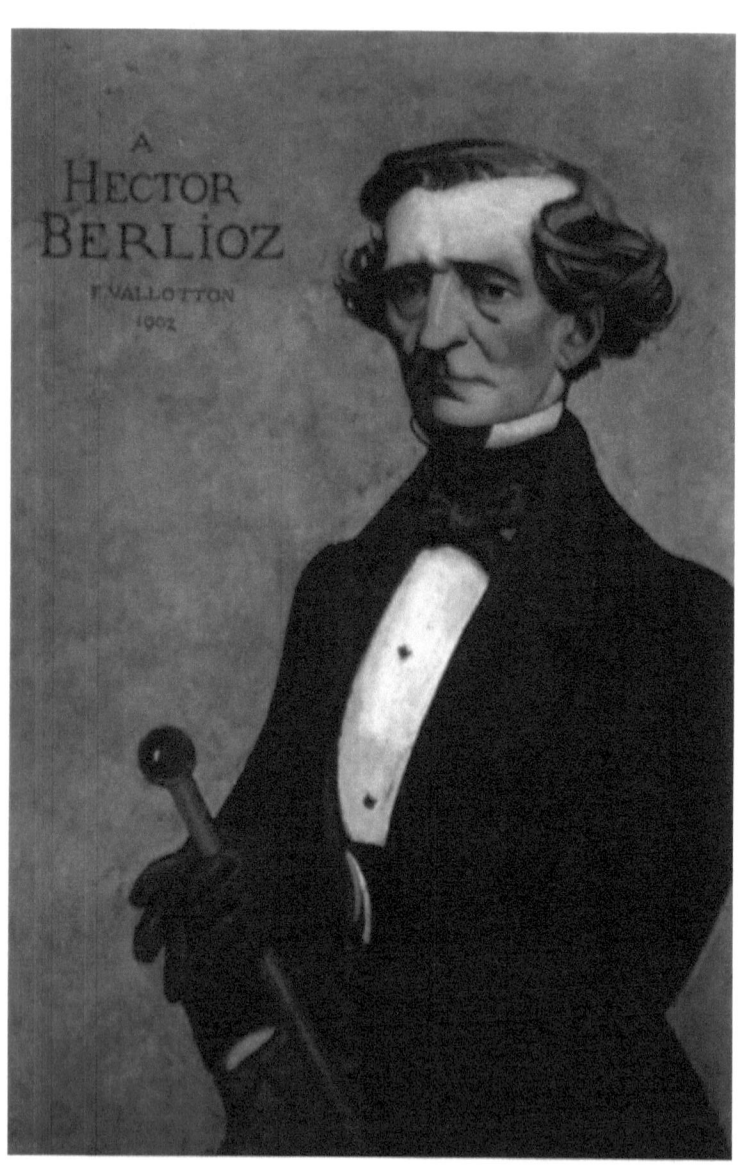

Portrait of Berlioz, 1902, oil on canvas

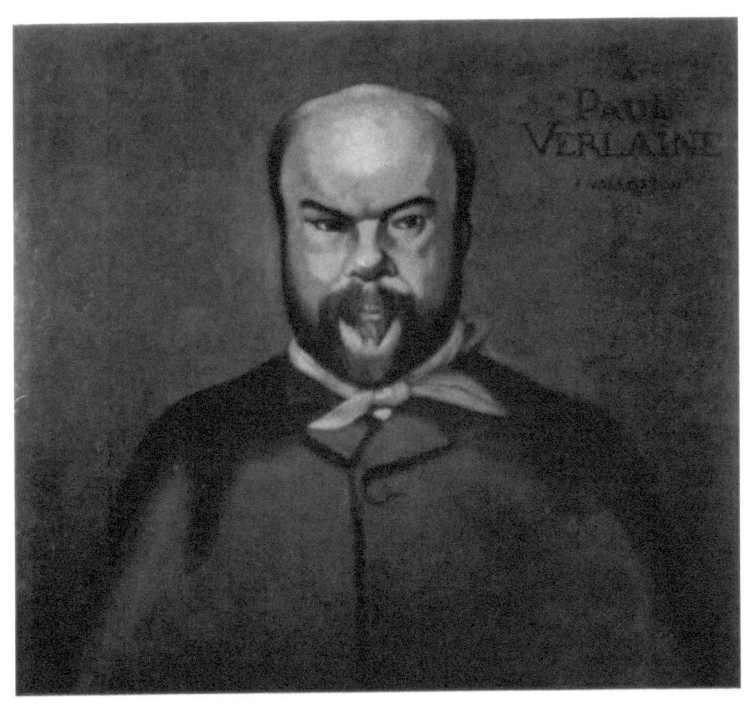

Portrait of Verlaine, 1902, oil on canvas

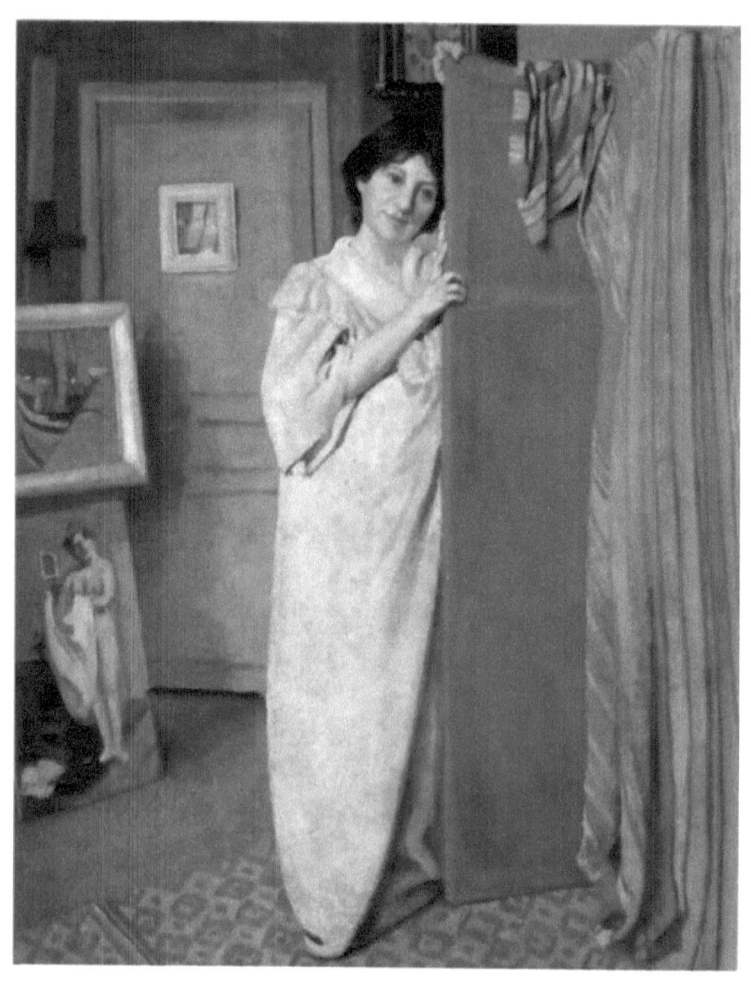

Portrait of workshop with figure (my wife), 1902, oil on canvas

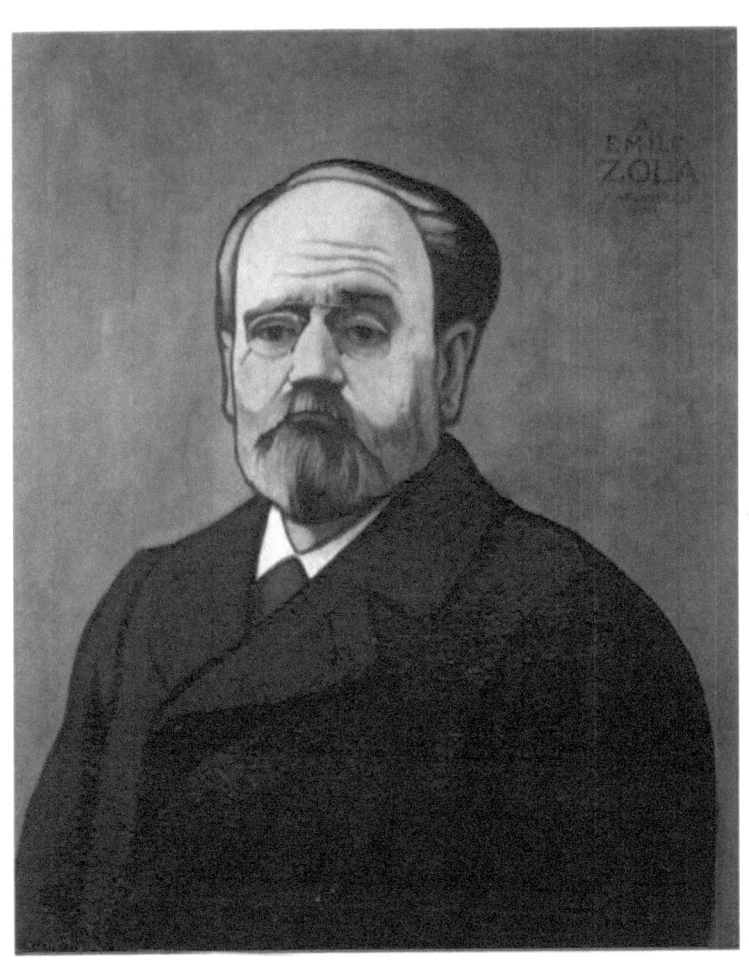

Portrait of Zola, 1902, oil on canvas

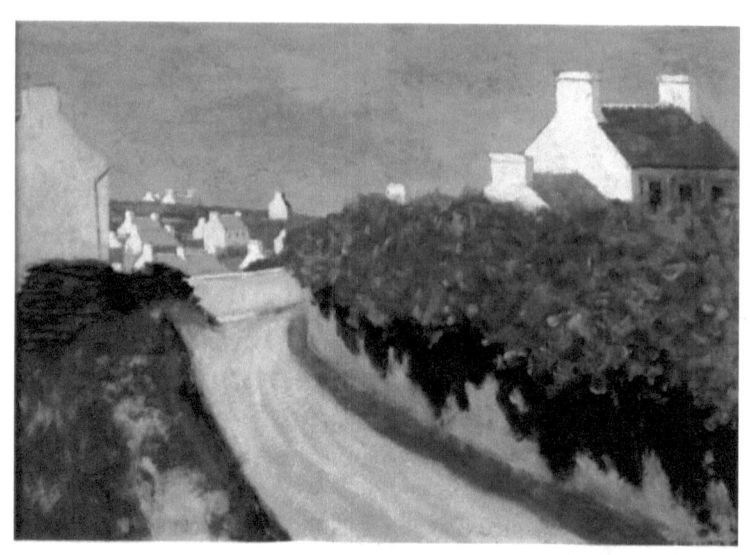

The Way to Locquirec, 1902, oil on canvas

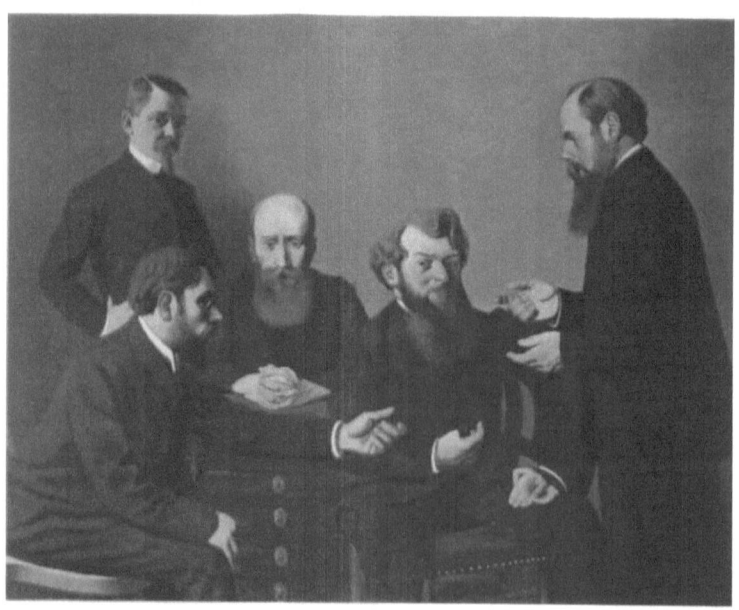

The Five Painters: Bonnard, Vuillard, Roussel, Cottet
and Vallotton, 1902, oil on canvas

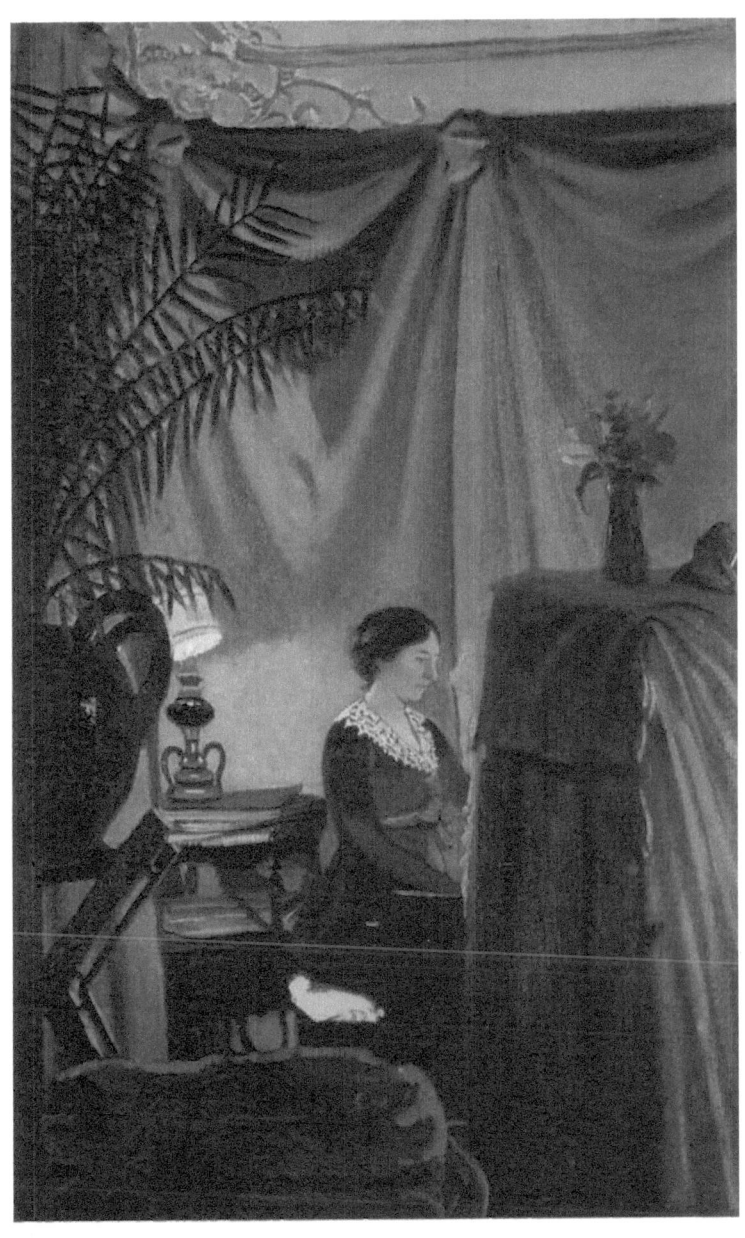

Gabrielle Vallotton at the Piano, 1904, oil on canvas

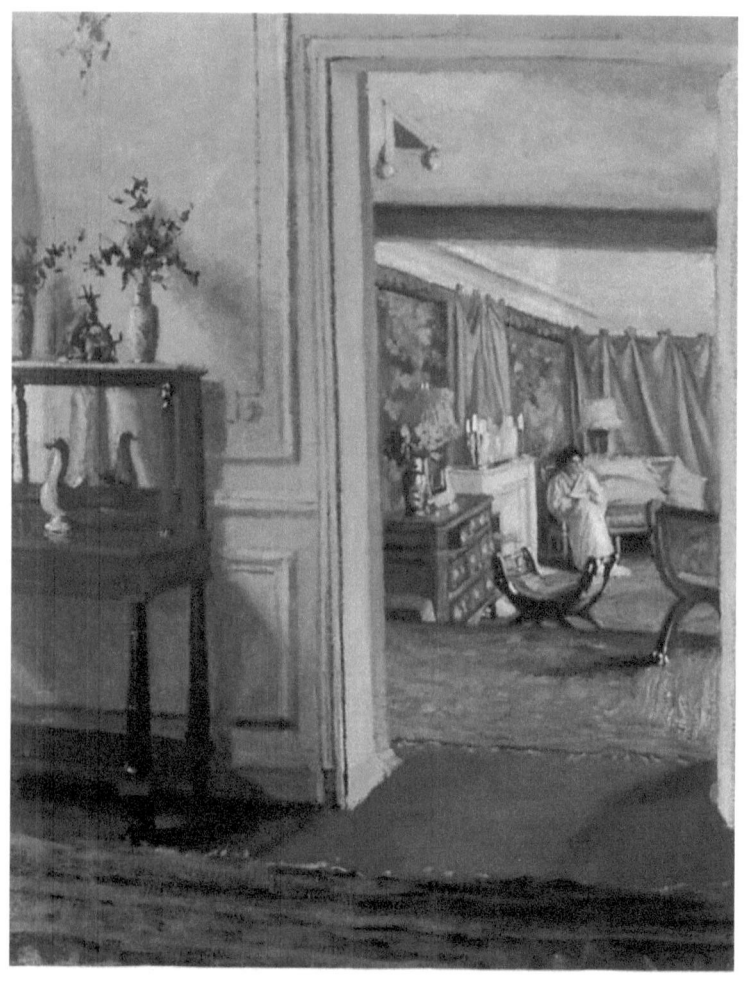

Interior with Woman in Pink, 1903-1904, oil on canvas

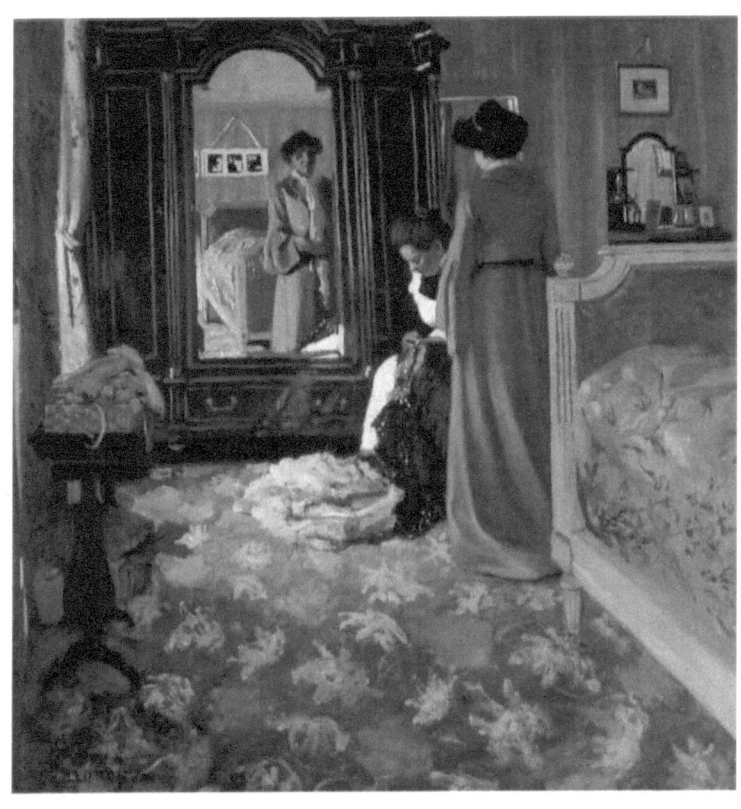

Interior, Bedroom with Two Figures, 1903-1904, oil on canvas

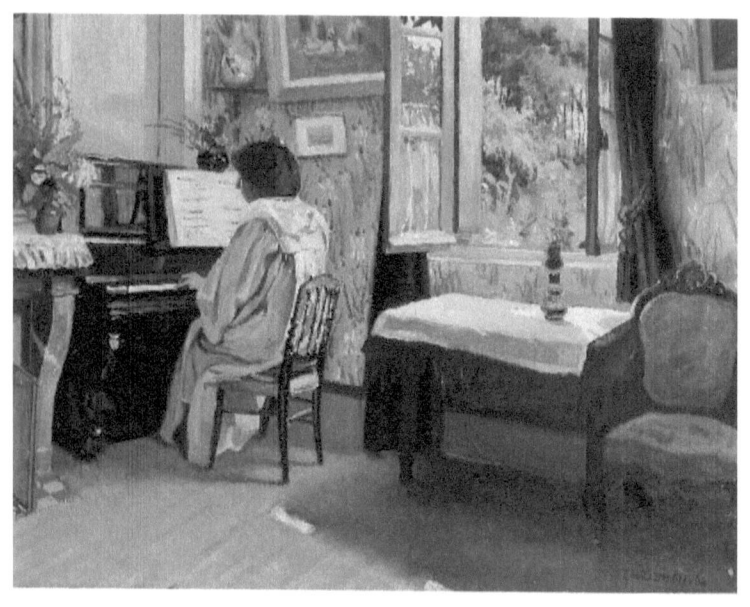

Lady at the Piano, 1904, oil on canvas

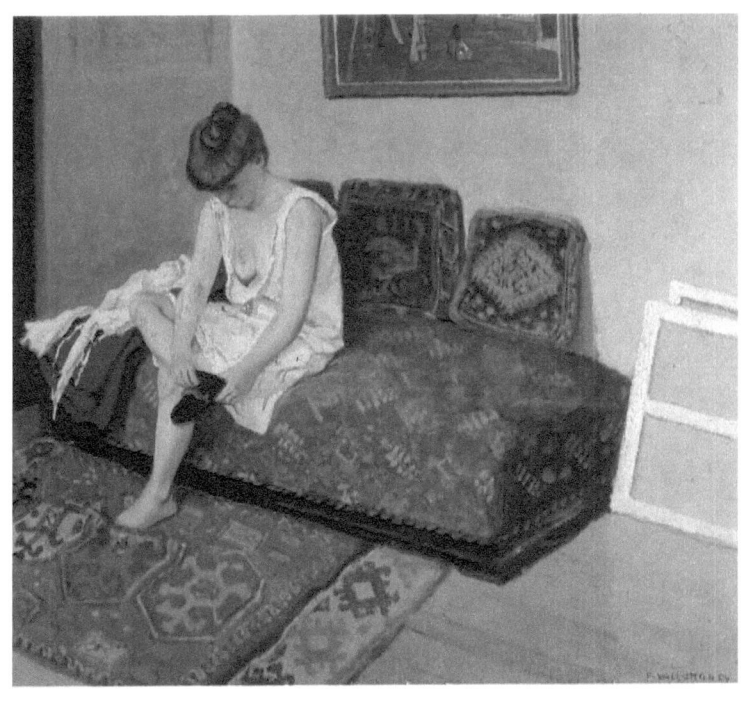

The Black Stocking, 1904, oil on canvas

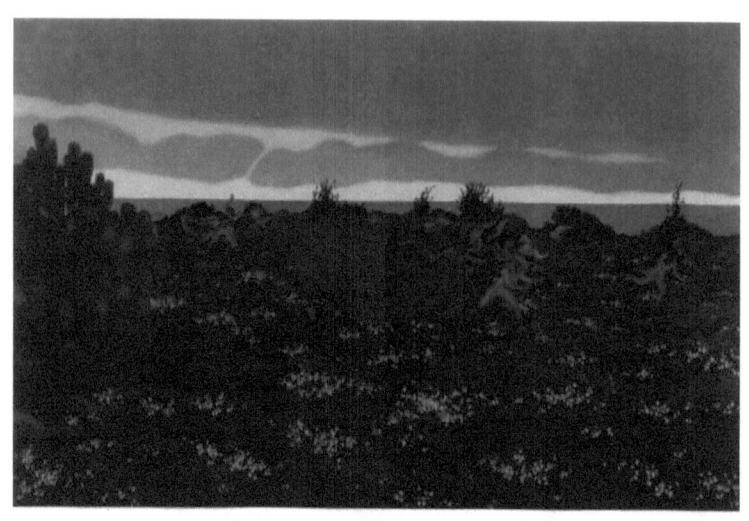

Twilight, 1904, oil

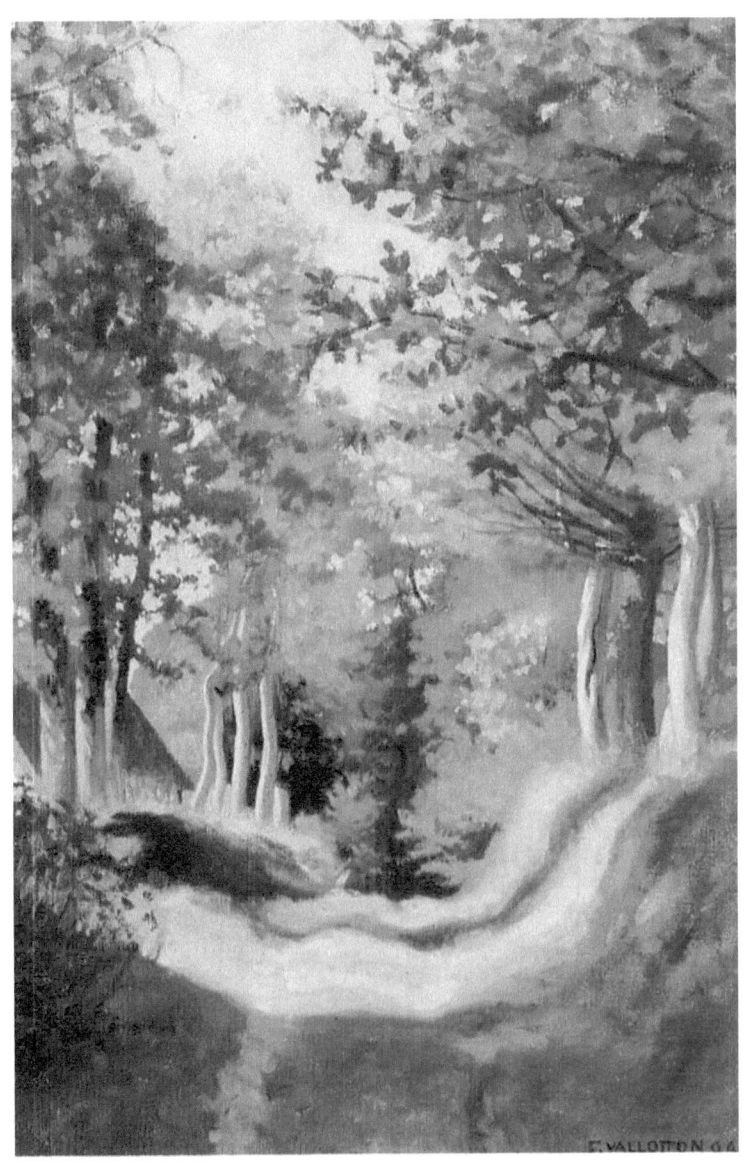

Undergrowth, 1904, oil on canvas

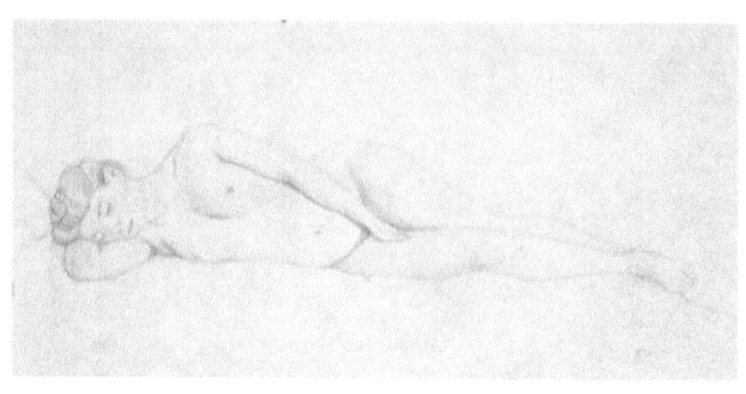

Reclining Female Nude, c.1905, pencil

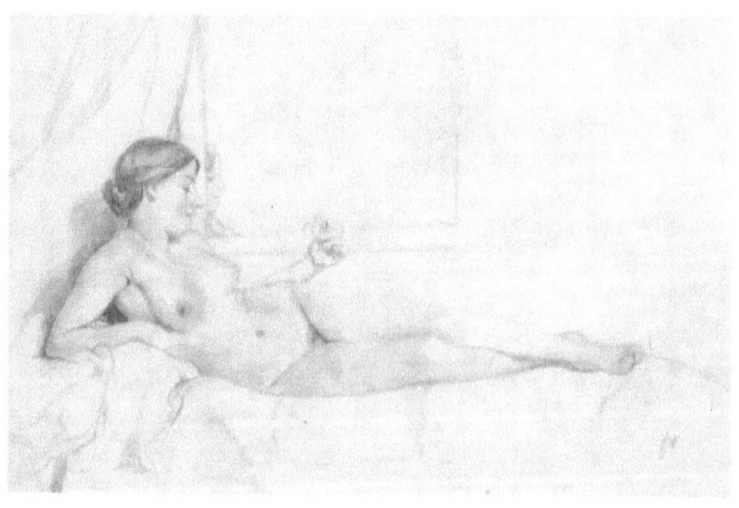

Reclining Nude on a couch, c.1905, pencil

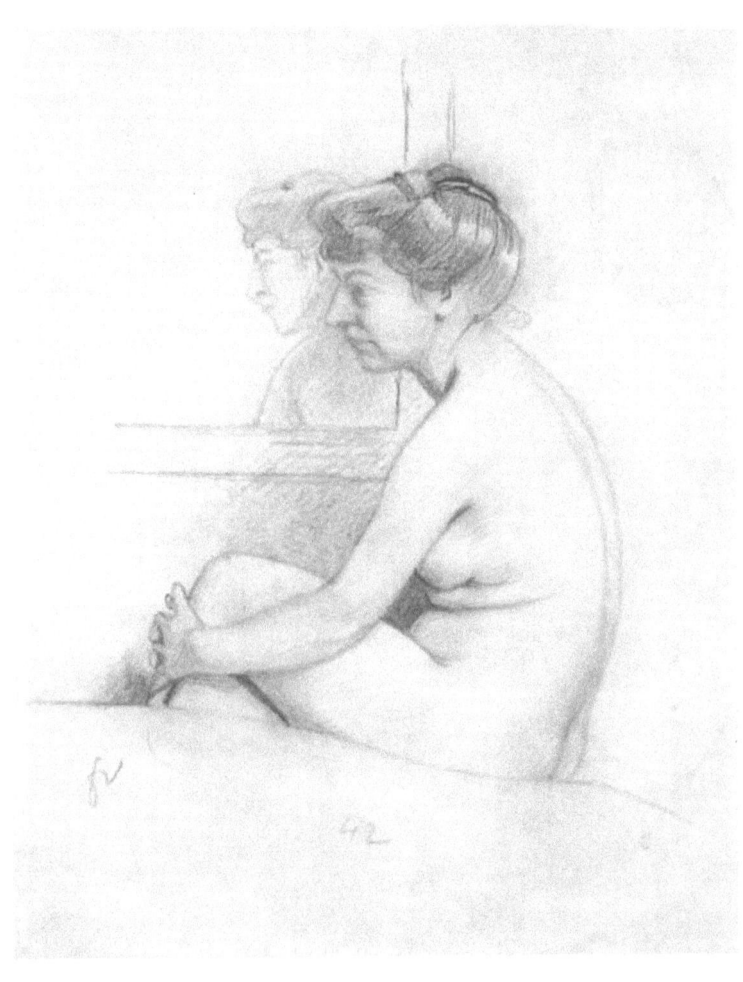

Seated Nude on a couch, c.1905, pencil

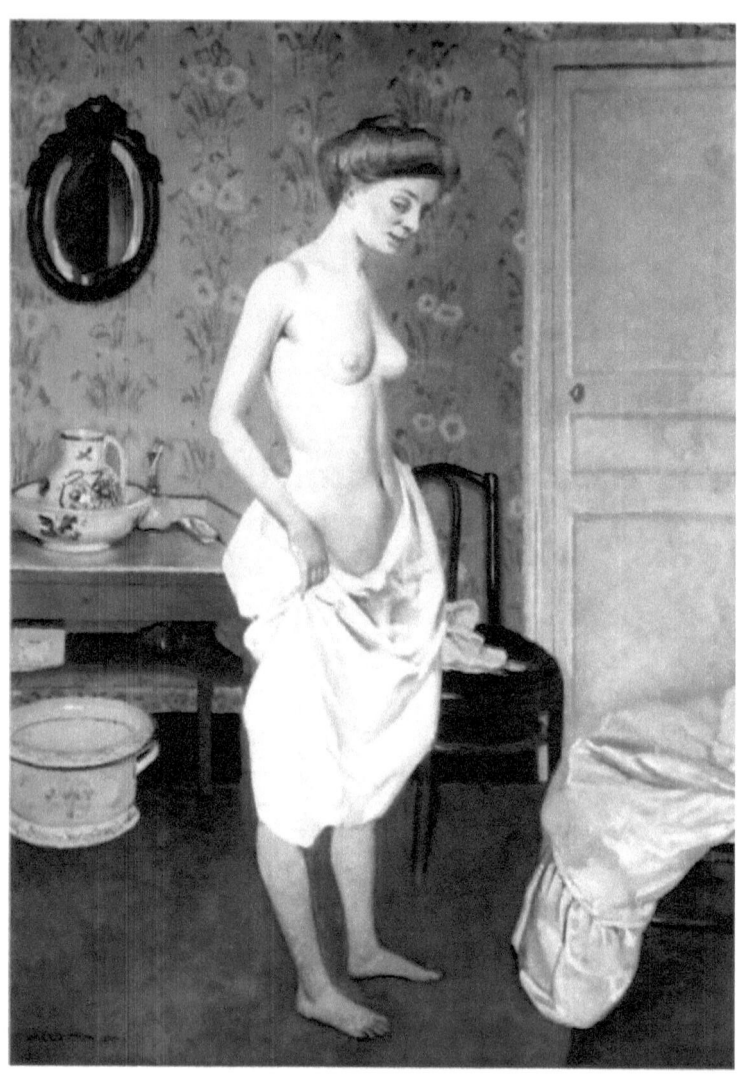

The Toilet, 1905, oil on canvas

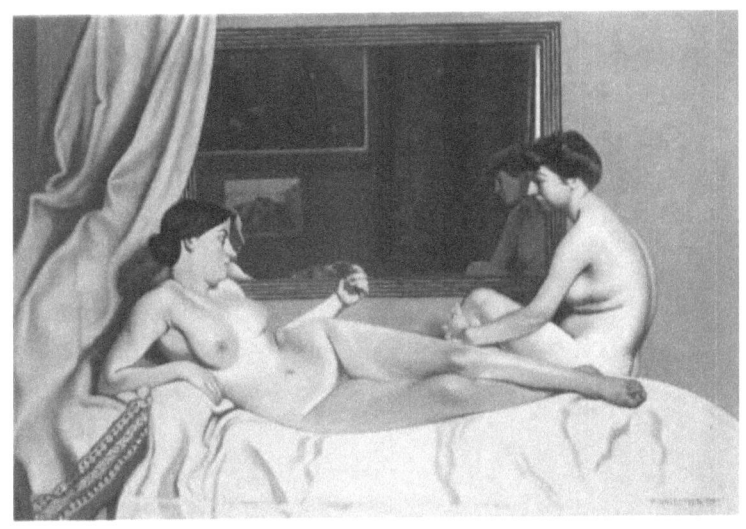

The rest of the models , 1905, oil on canvas

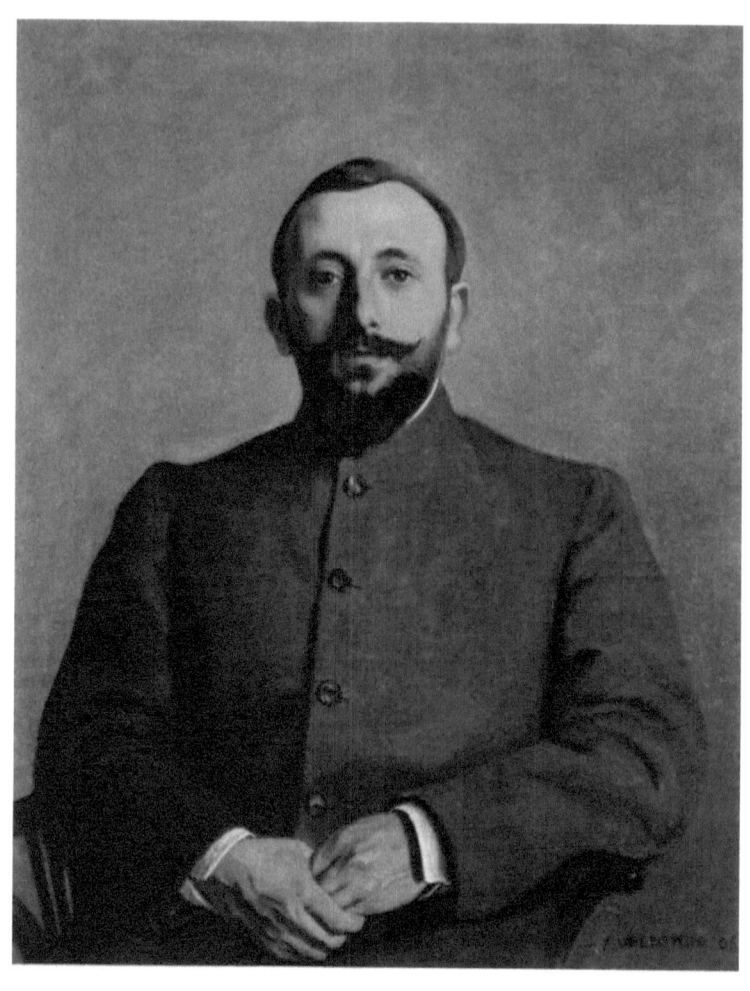

Alfred Athis (Pseudonym of Alfred Natanson), 1906, oil on canvas

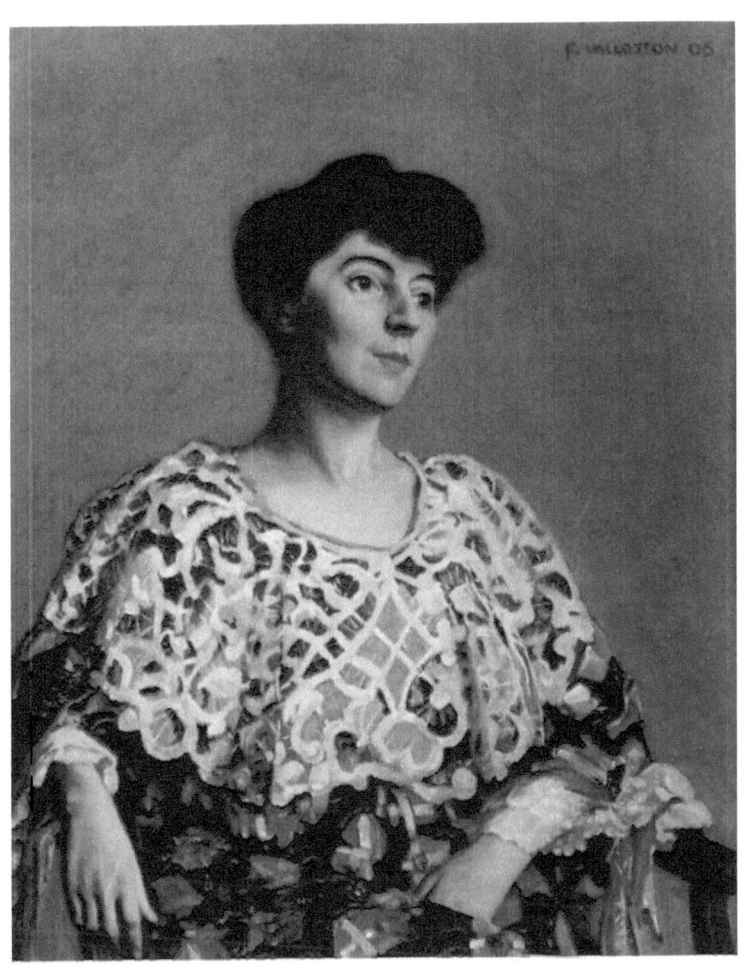

Marthe Mellot (wife of Alfred Natanson), 1906, oil on canvas

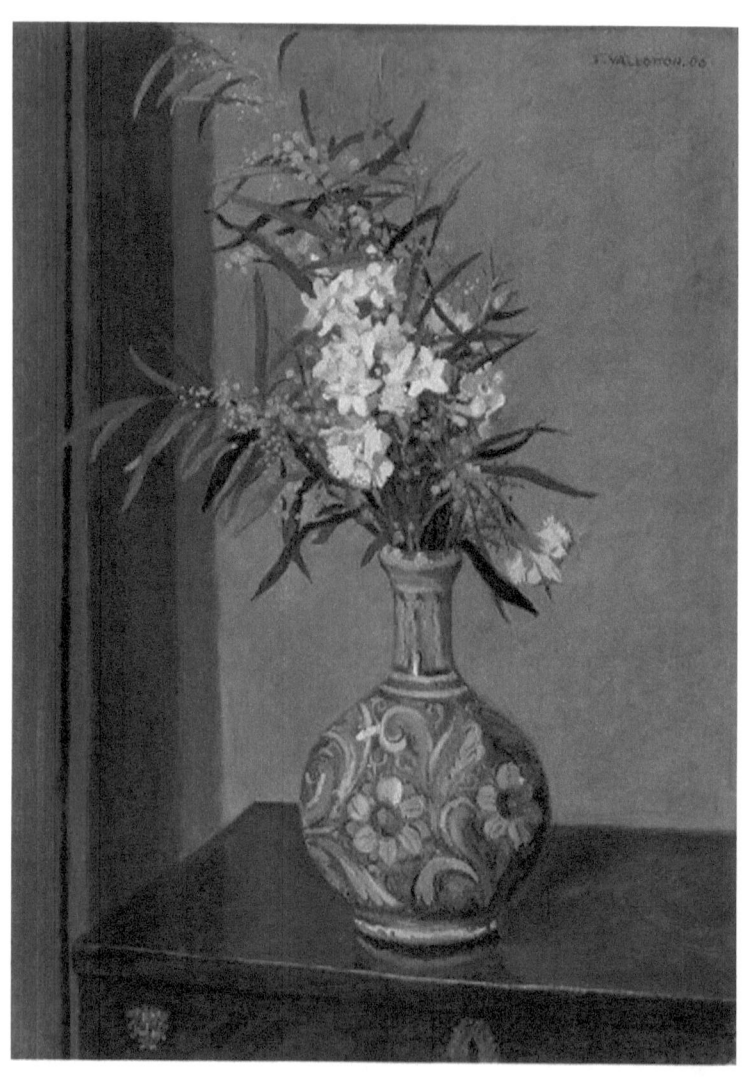

White flowers in a vase decorated, 1906, oil on canvas

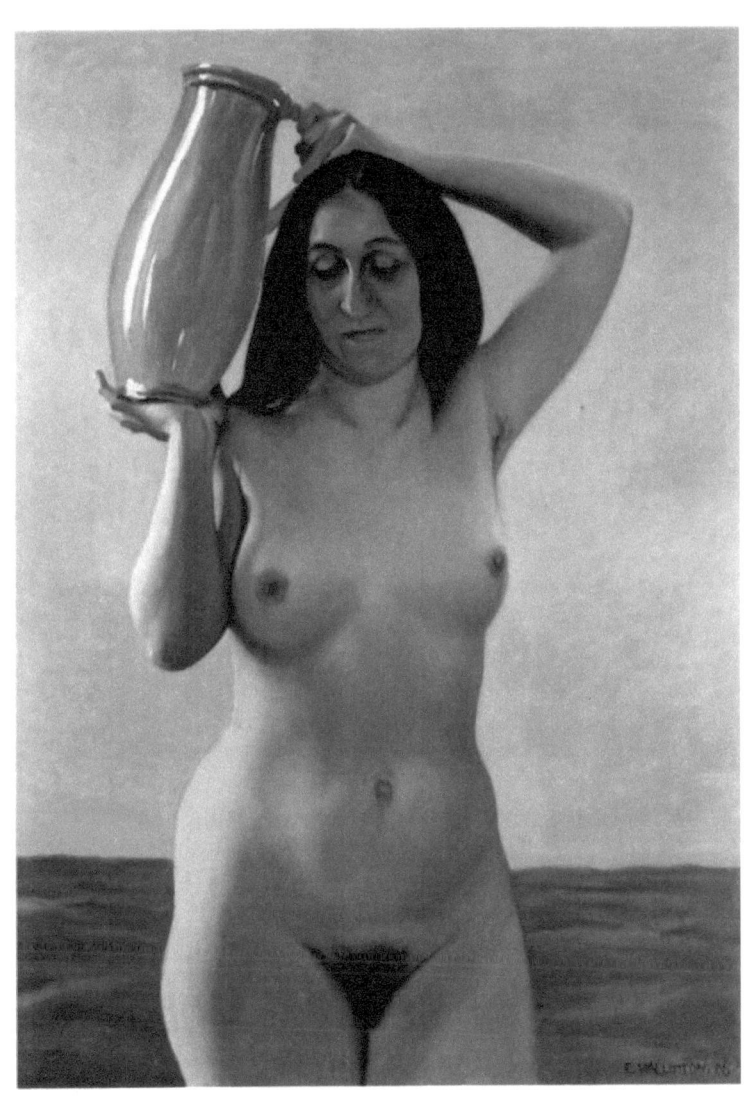

Woman with the Jug, 1906, oil

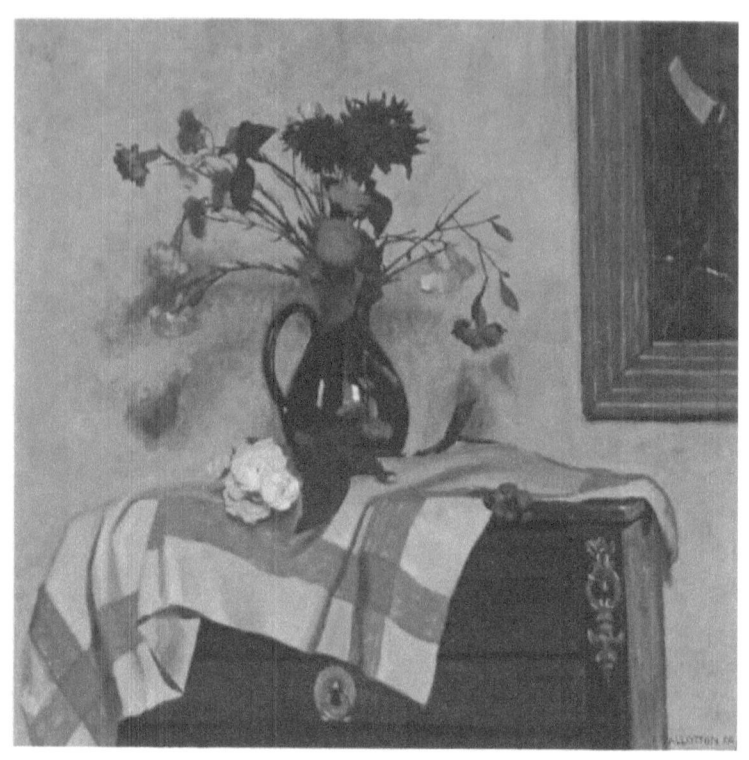

Still Life with Self-portrait, 1906, oil

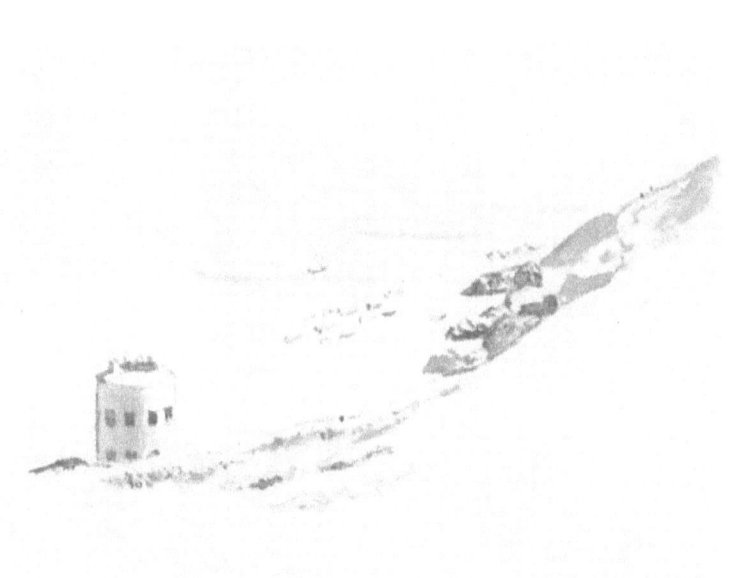

Martello tower in Guernsey, 1907, watercolor

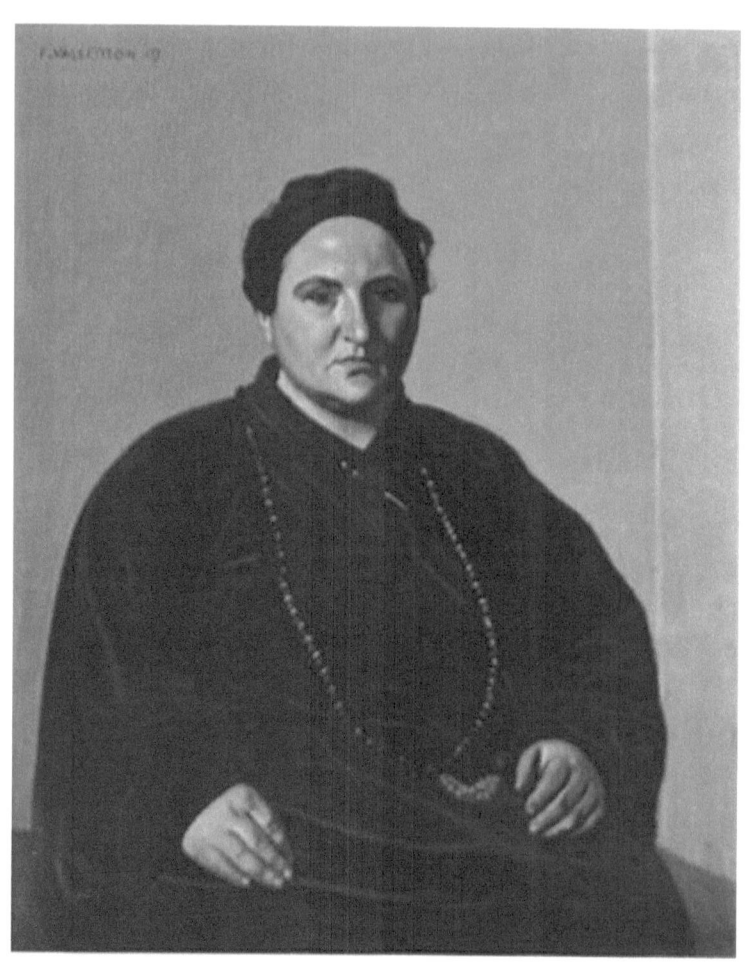

Portrait of Gertrude Stein, 1907, oil

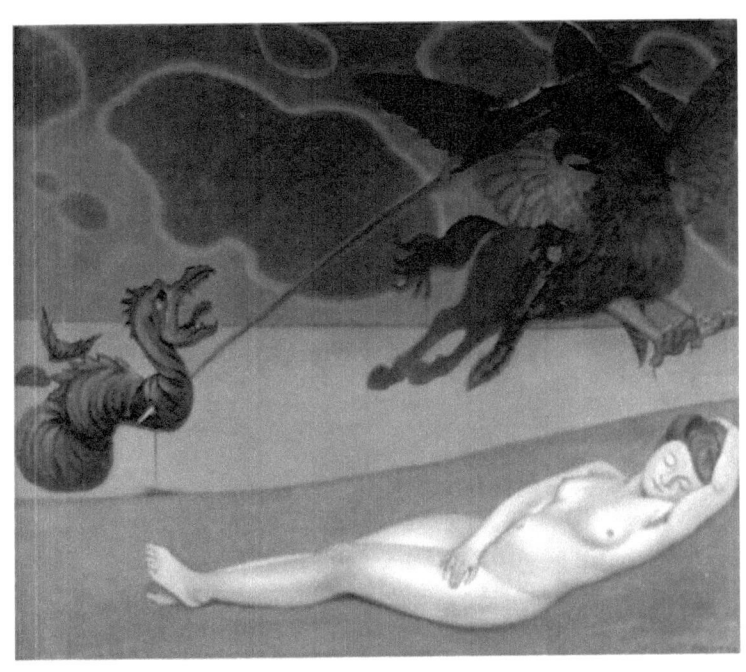

Roger delivering Angelica, 1907, oil on canvas

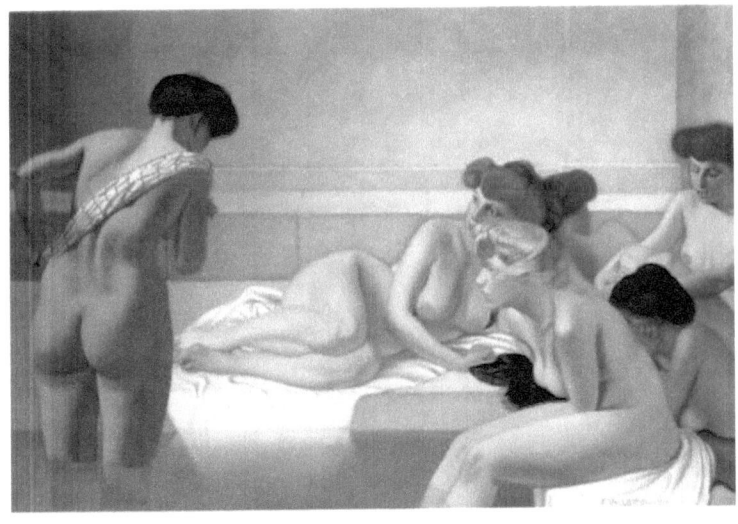

The Turkish bath, 1907, oil on canvas

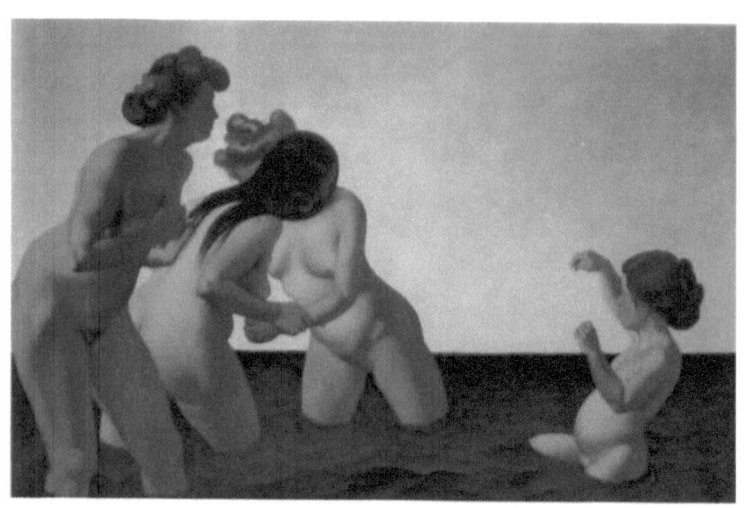

Three Women and a Little Girl Playing in the Water,
1907, oil on canvas

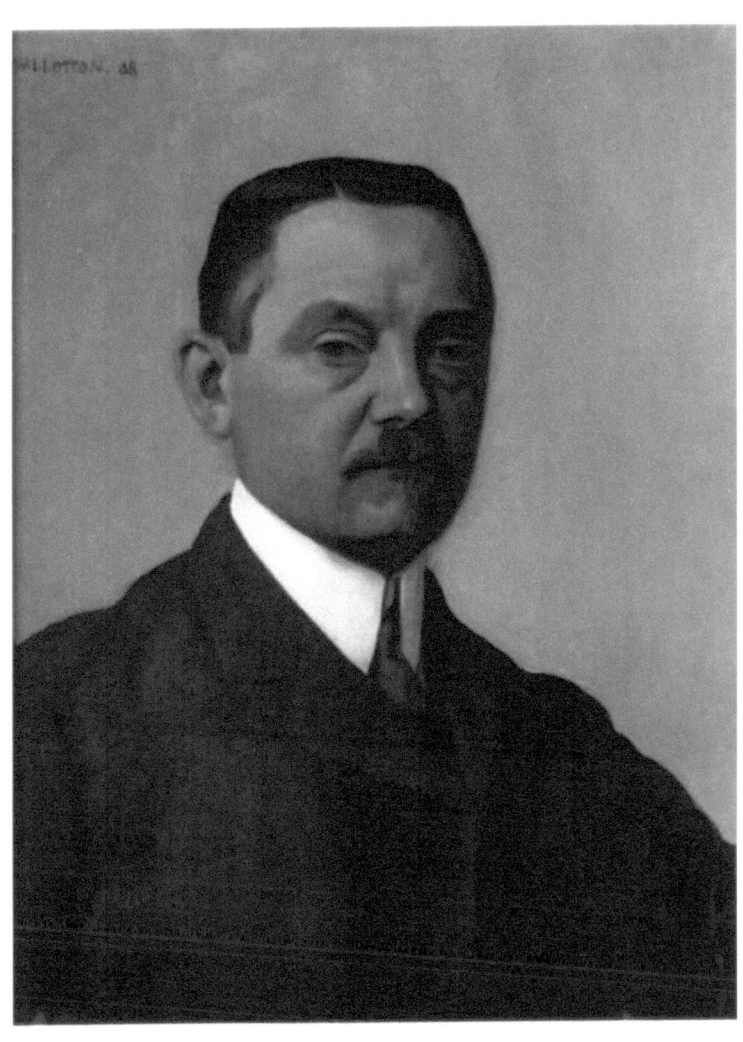

My portrait, 1908, oil on canvas

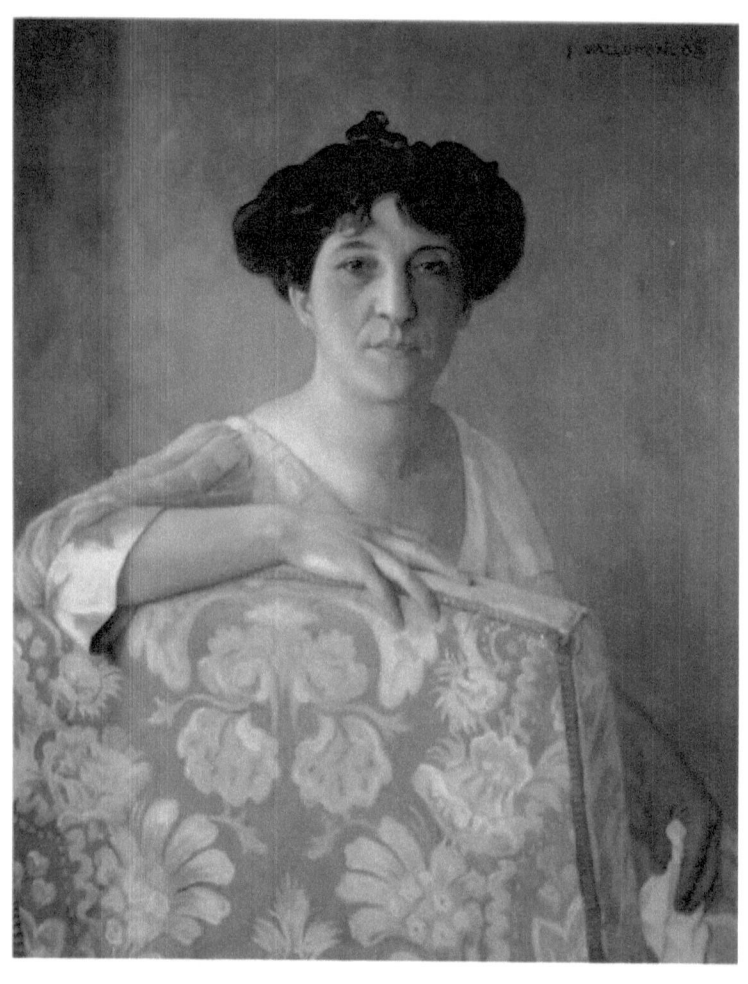

Portrait de Gabrielle Vallotton, 1908, oil on canvas

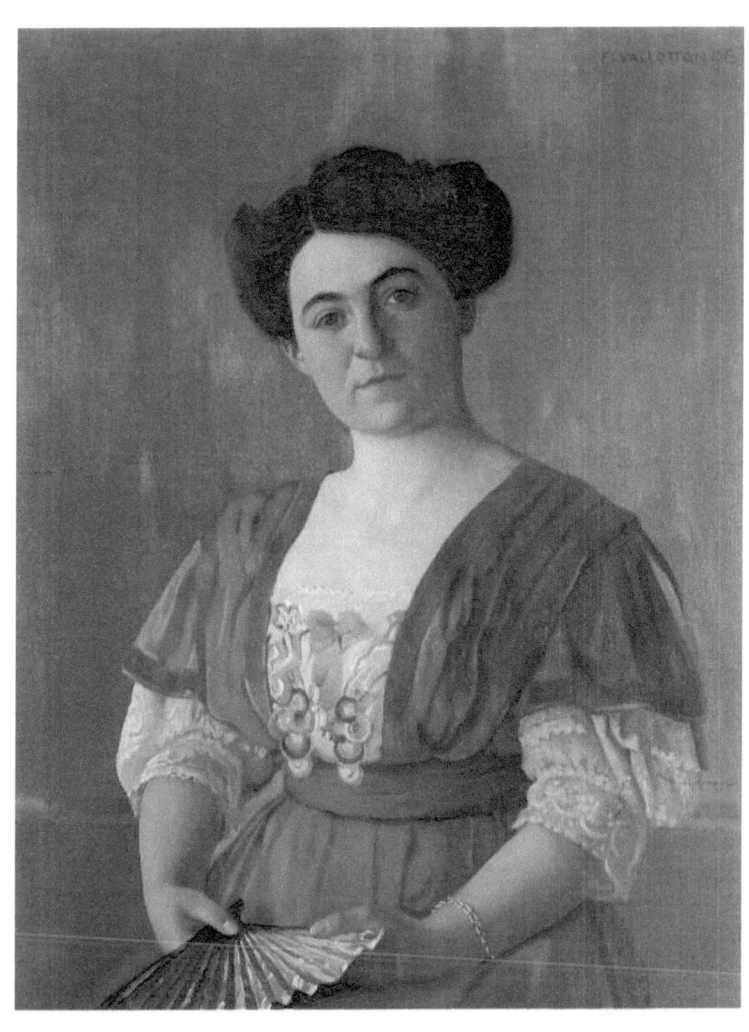

Portrait of Madame Hasen, 1908, oil on canvas

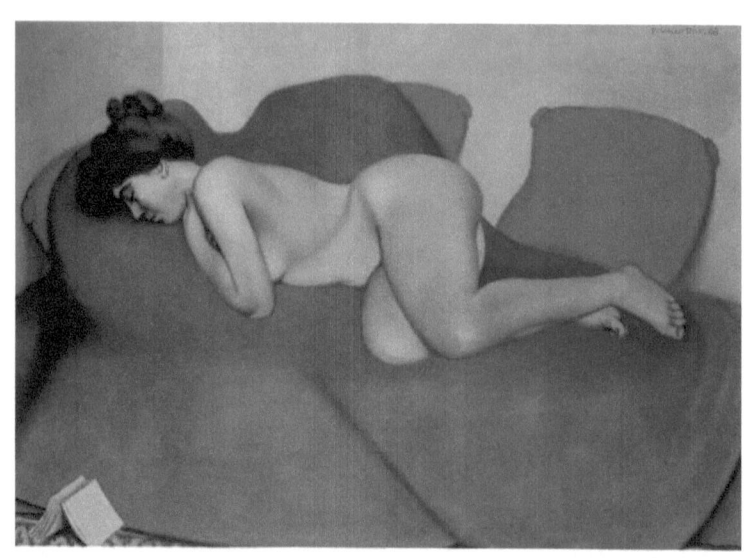

Sleep, 1908, oil on canvas

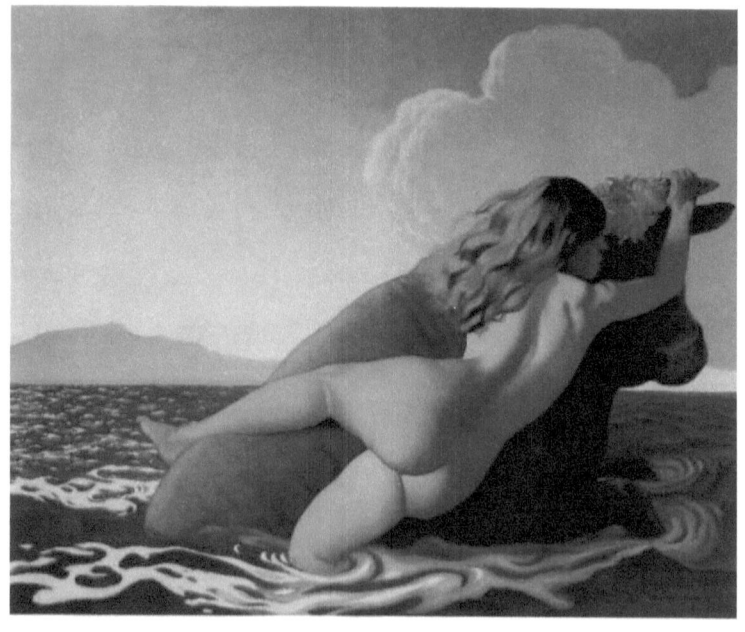

The Rape of Europa, 1908, oil

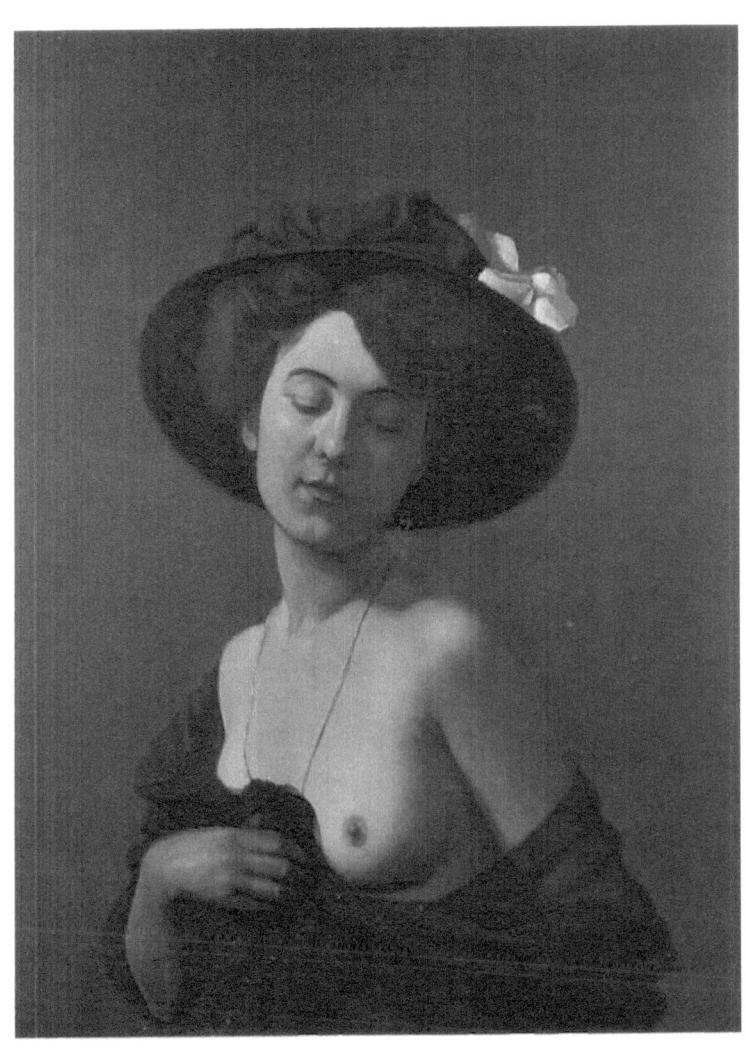

Woman with a Black Hat, 1908, oil on canvas

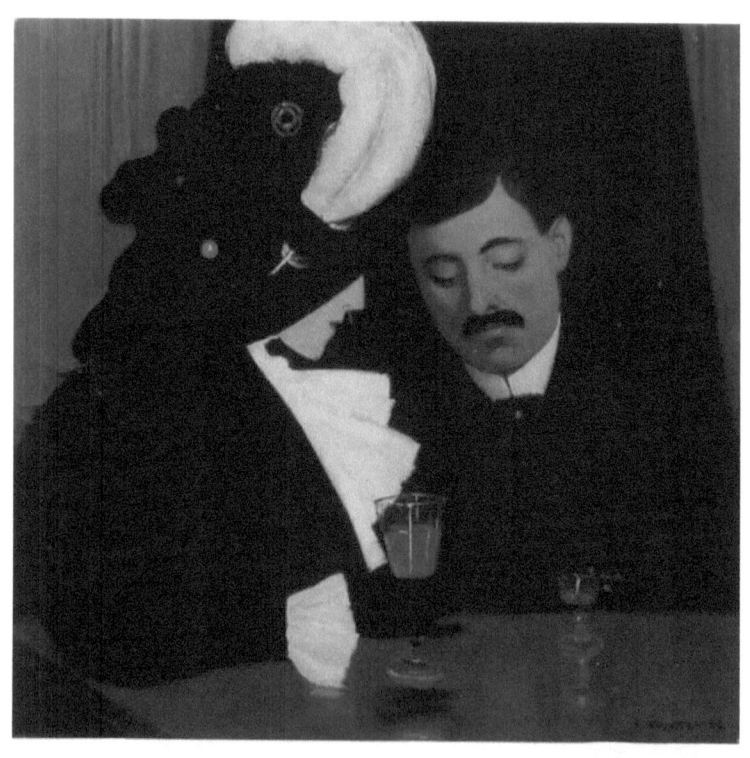

At the Cafe (also known as The Provincial), 1909, oil on canvas

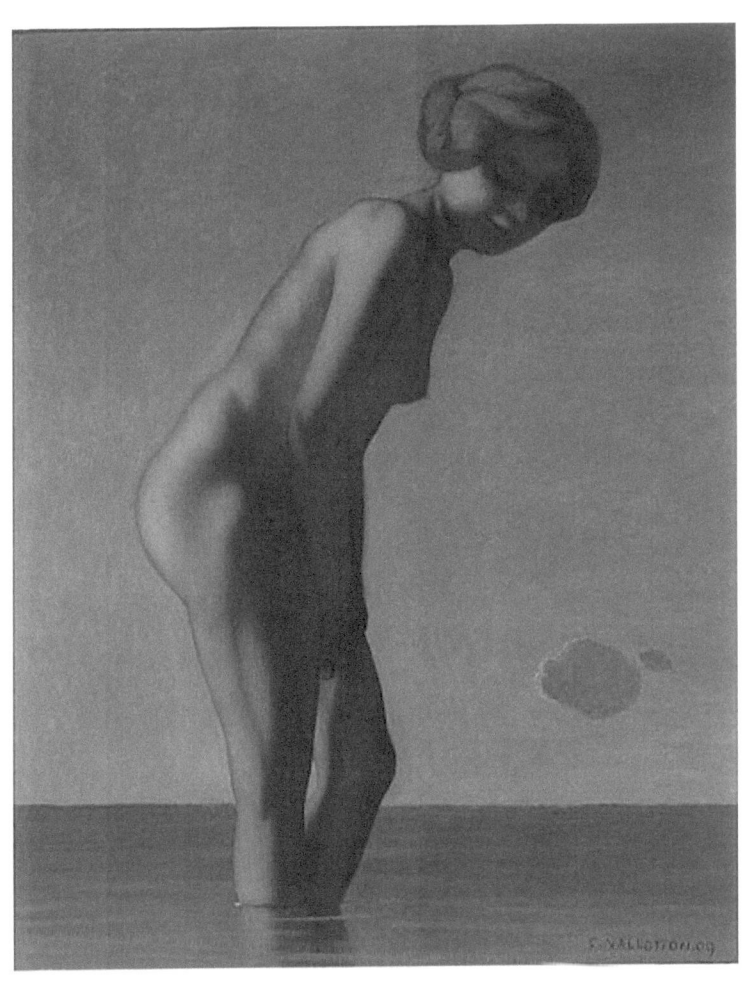

Bather looked to the right, 1909, oil

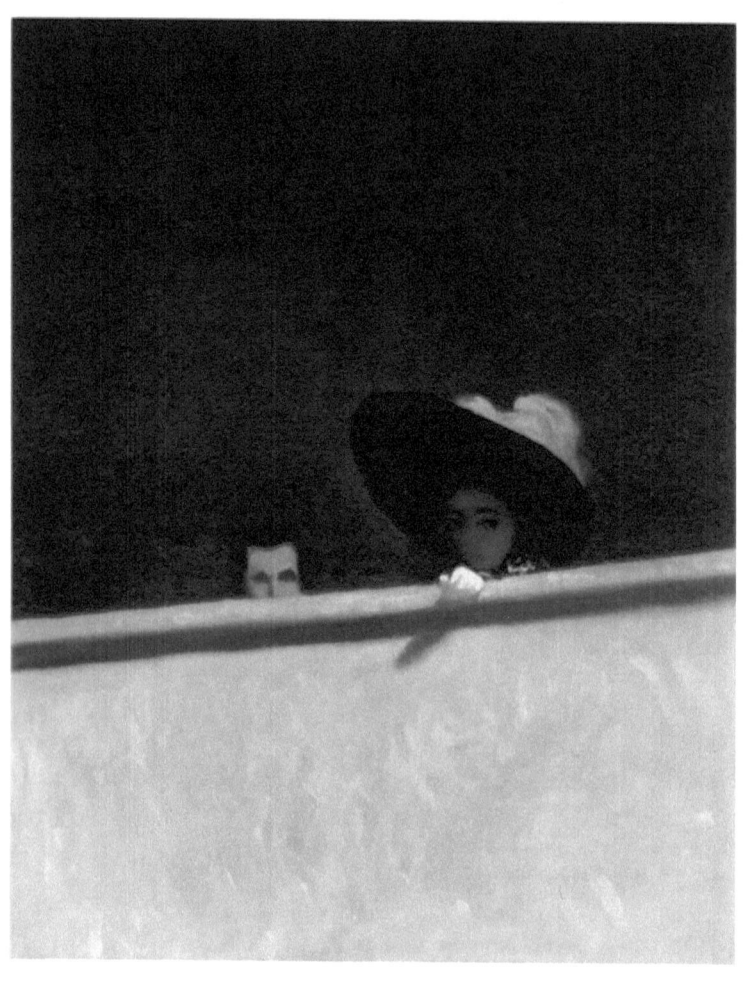

Box Seats at the Theater, the Gentleman and the Lady, 1909, oil

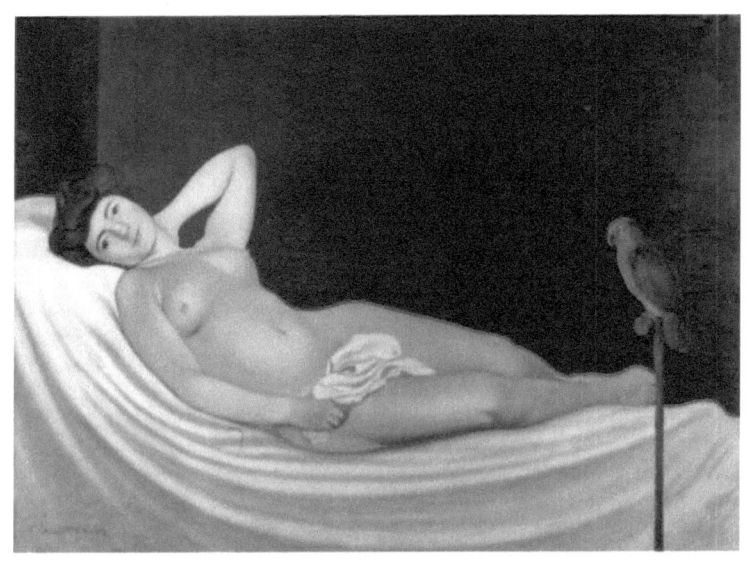

The Woman with the Parrot, 1909, oil on canvas

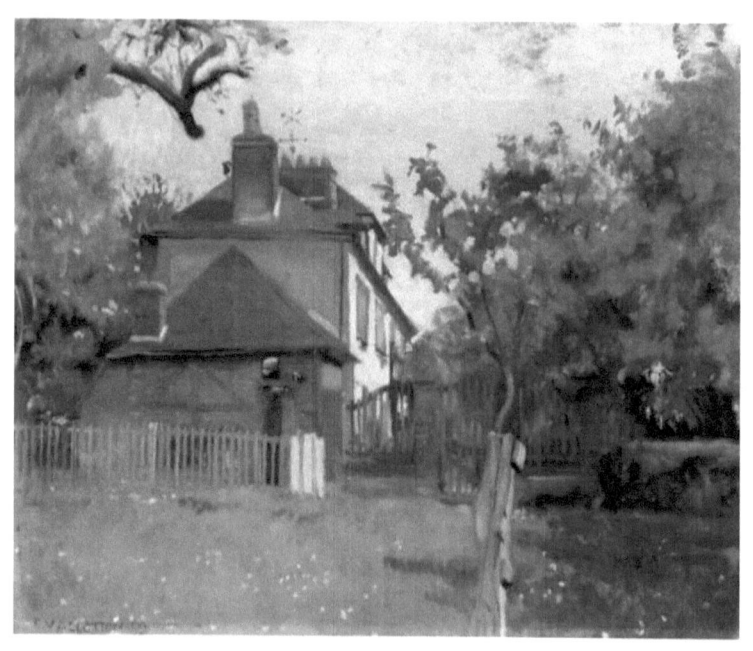

Villa Beaulieu, Honfleur, 1909, oil on canvas

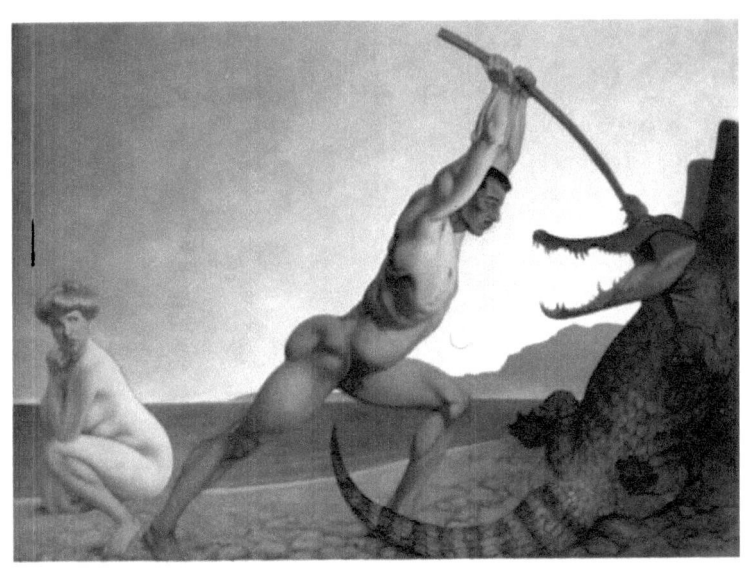

Persee killing the Dragon, 1910, oil on canvas

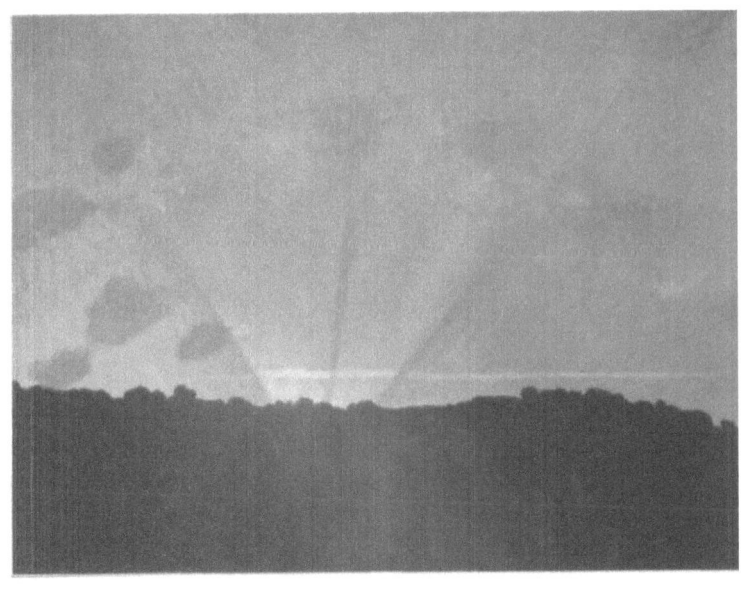

Sunset, 1910, oil on canvas

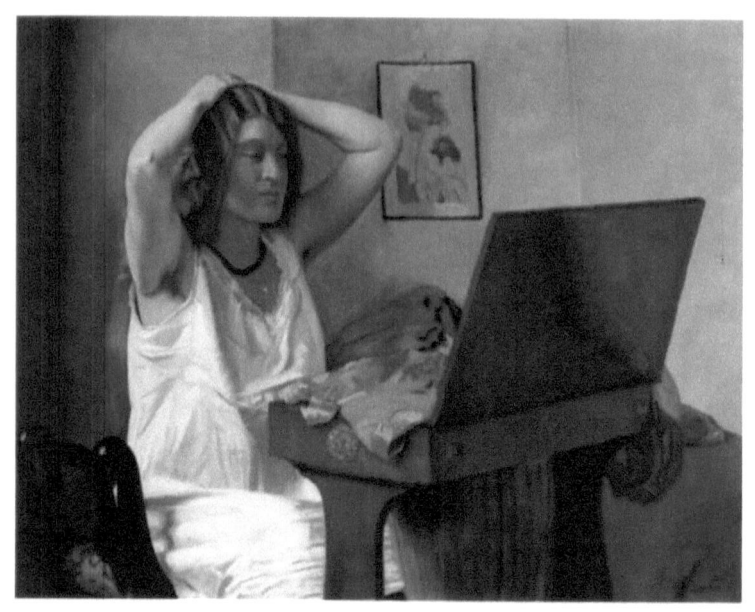

Coquettery, 1911, oil on canvas

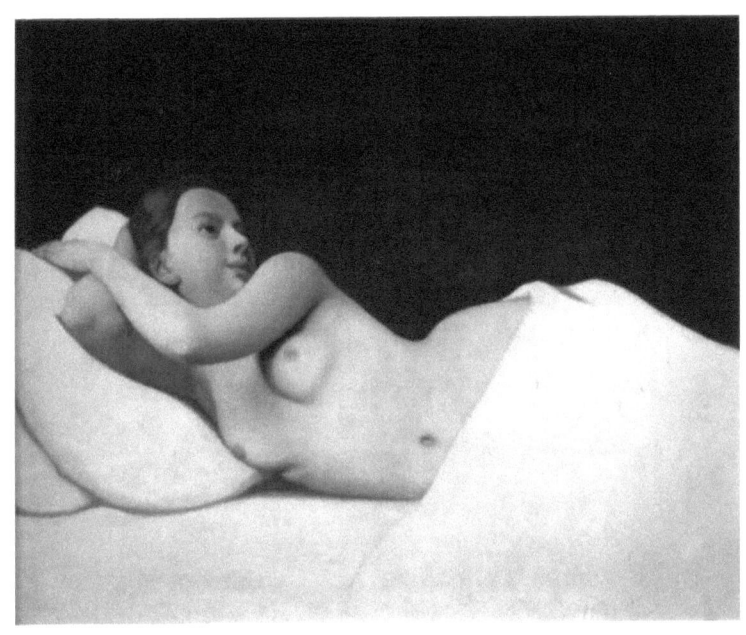

Rest, 1911, oil on canvas

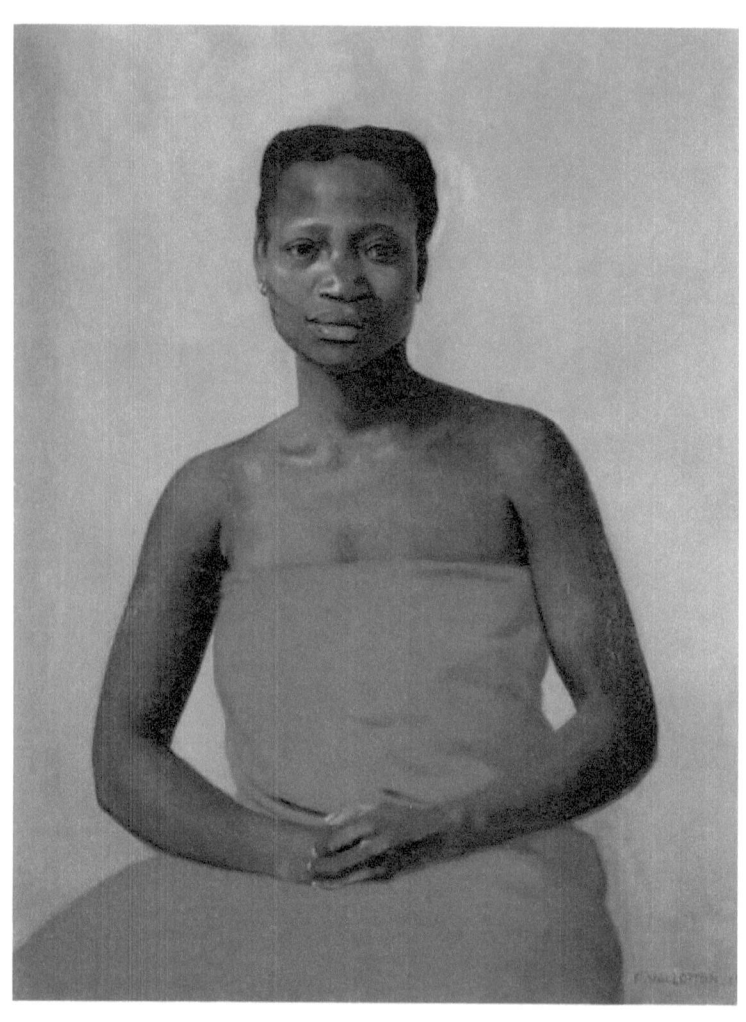

Seated Black Woman, Front View, 1911, oil on canvas

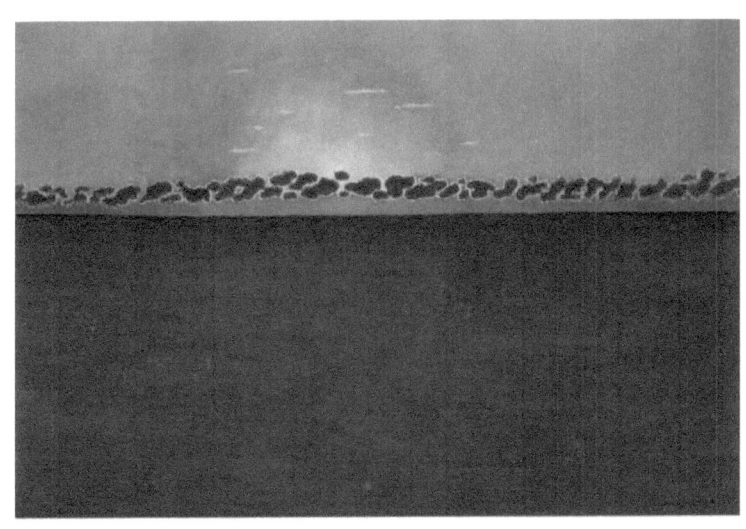

Sunset, Gray Blue High Tide, 1911, oil

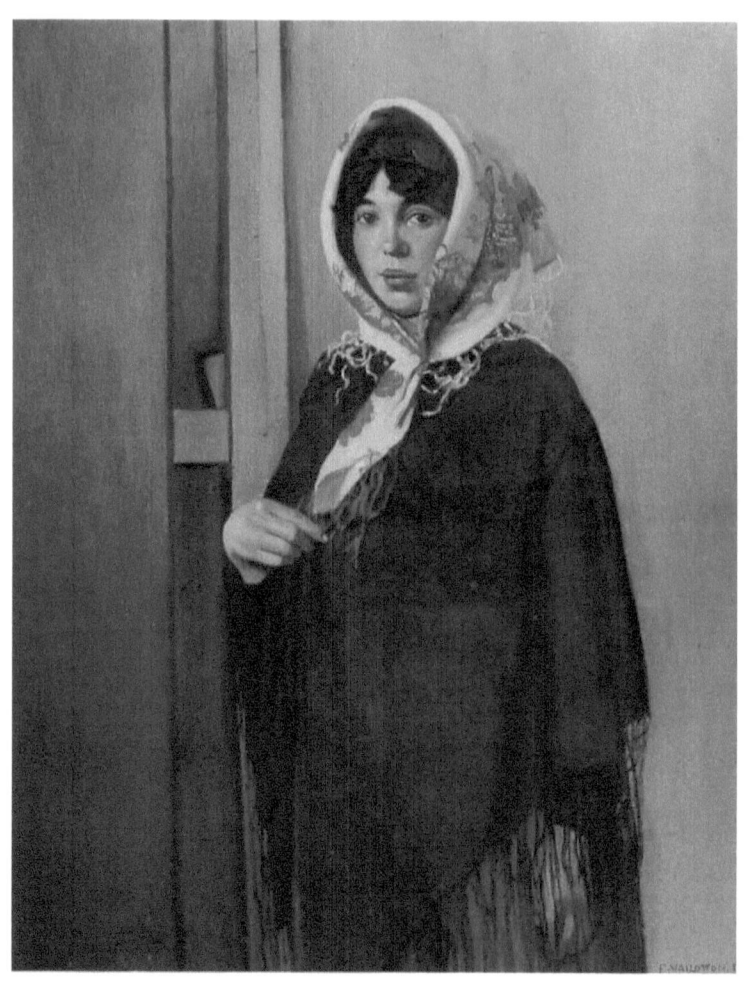

Young Woman with Yellow Scarf, 1911, oil on canvas

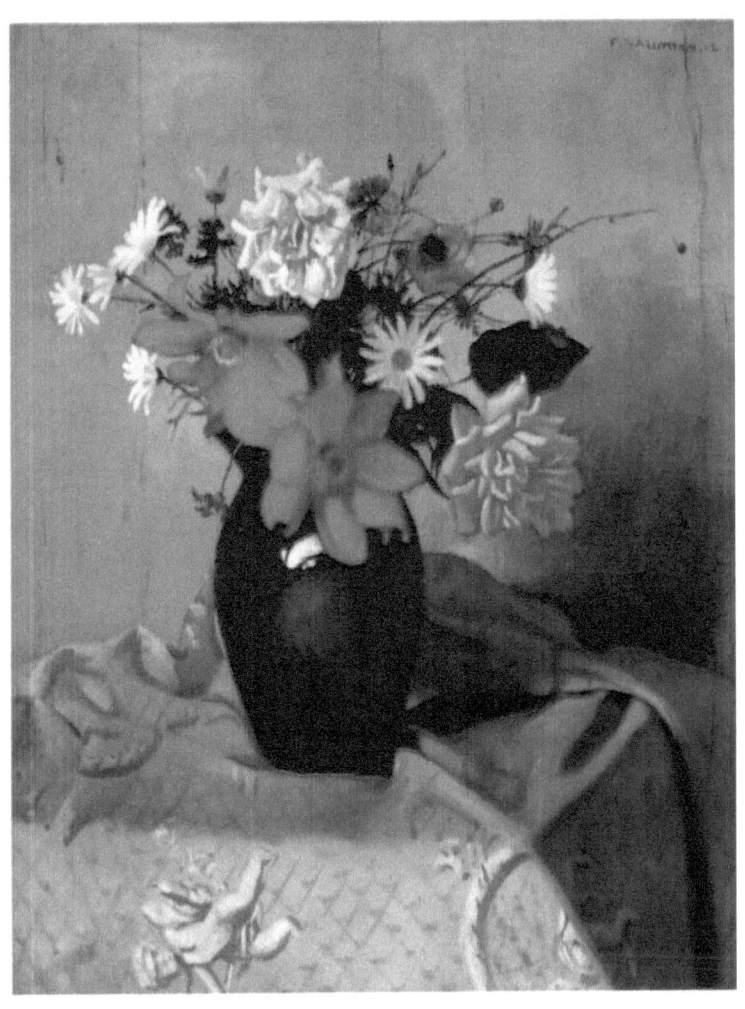

Pinks and daisies or Pinks and dahlias, 1912, oil on canvas

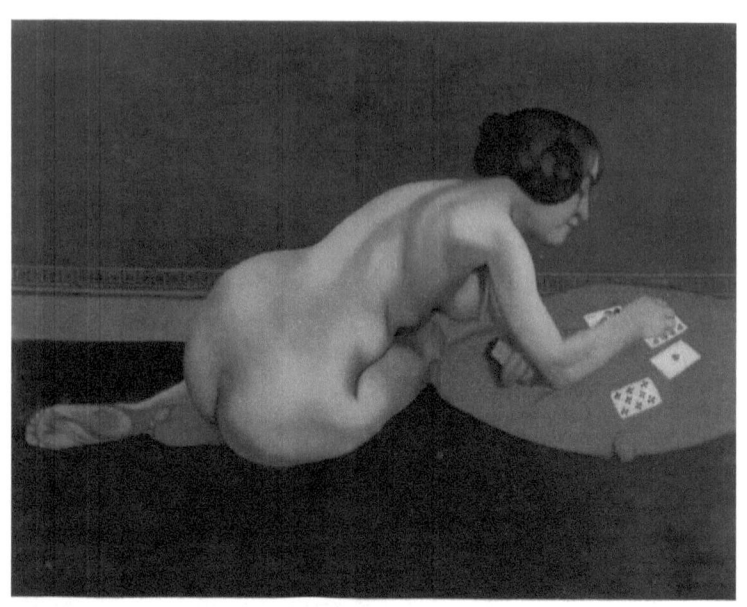

Solitaire (also known as Nude Playing Cards), 1912, oil on canvas

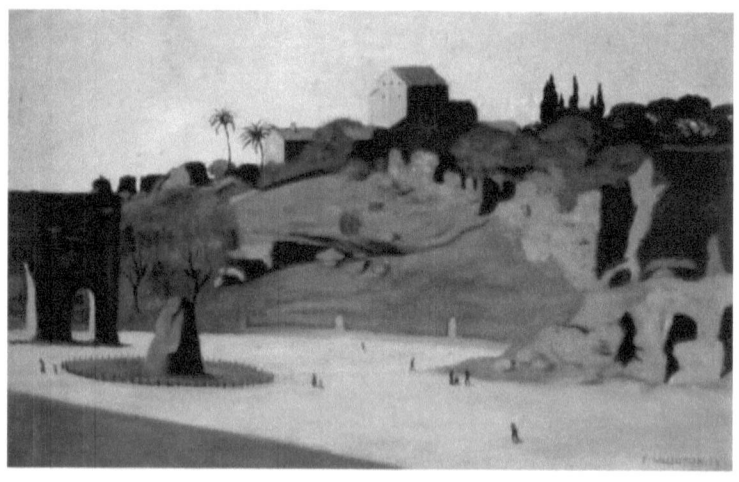

Forum Roman or Seen close the Palatine one, 1913, oil on canvas

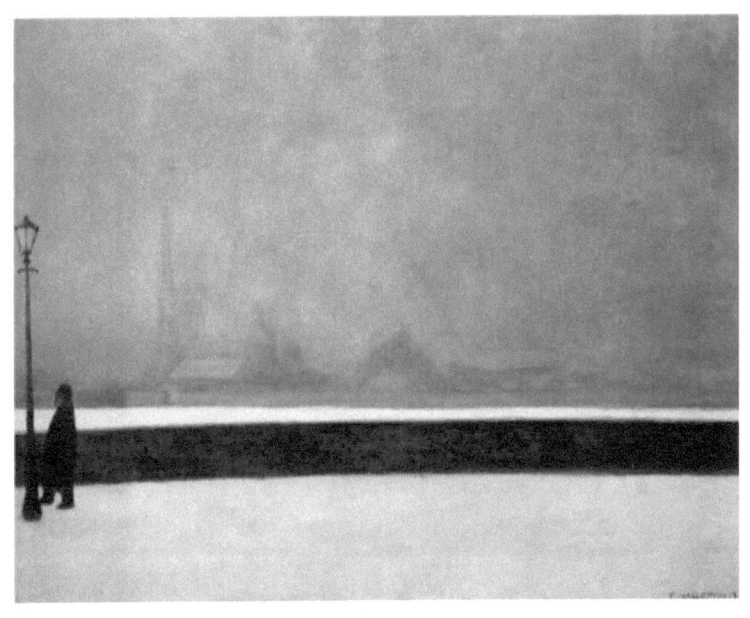

Neva, light fog, 1913, oil

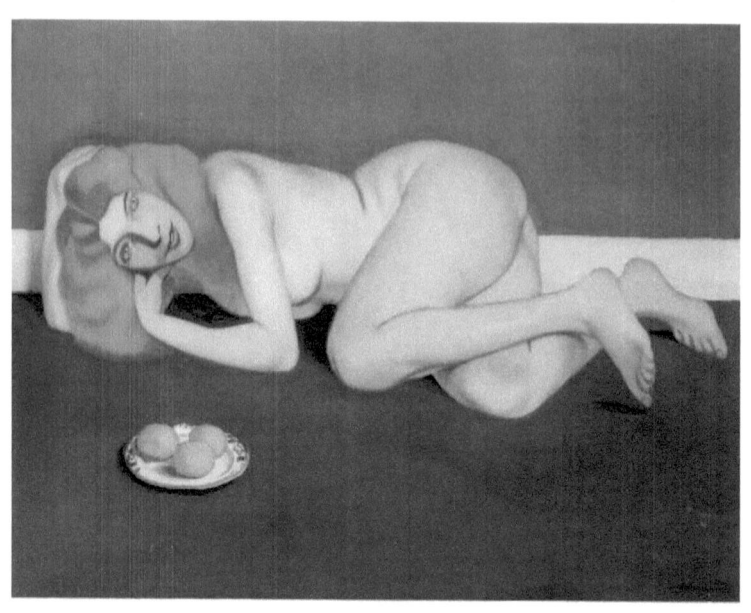

Nude Blond Woman with Tangerines, 1913, oil on
canvas

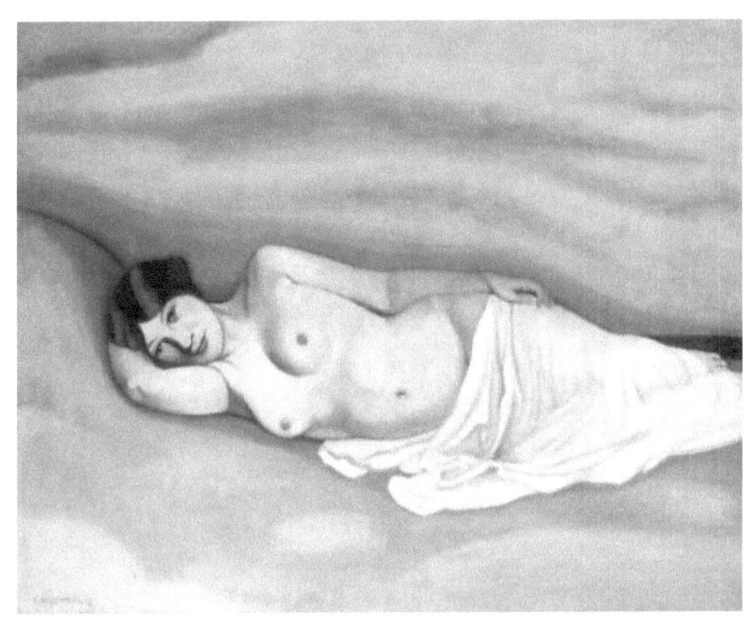

Nude in Bed, 1913, oil

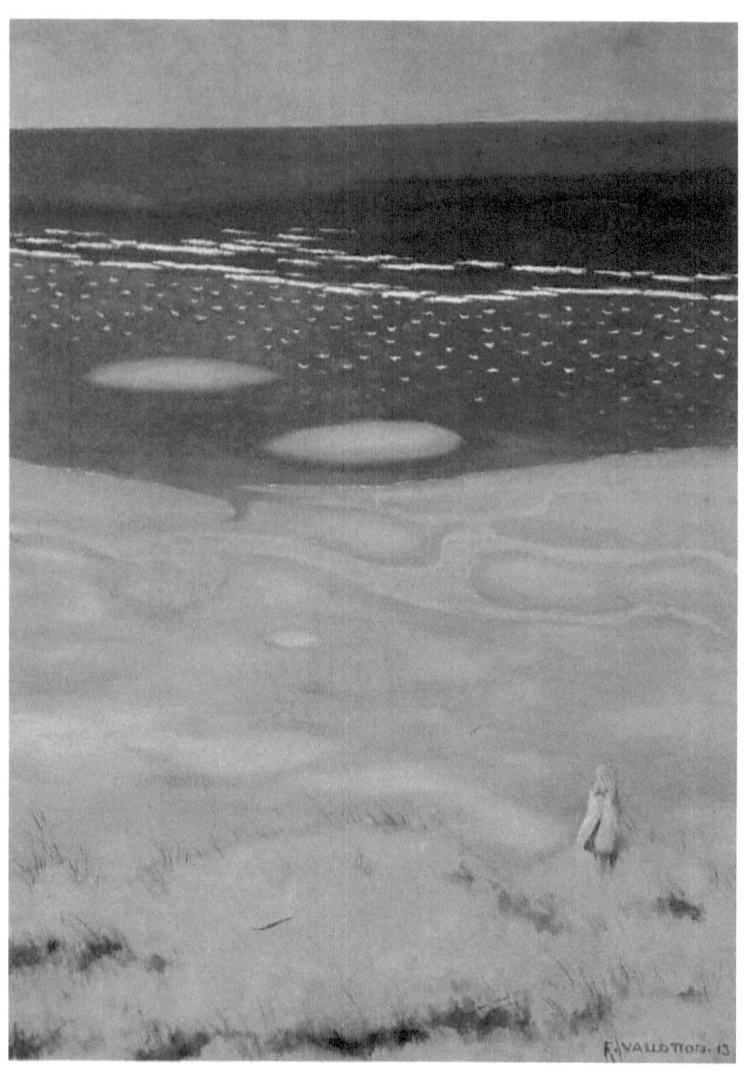

The Rising Tide, 1913, oil on canvas

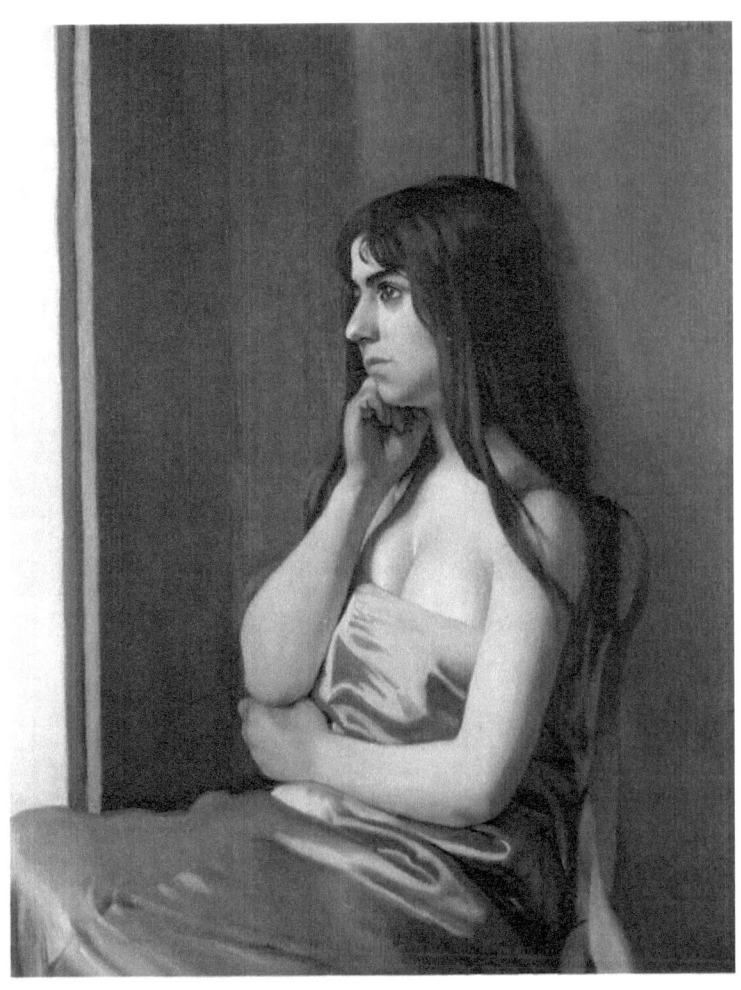

The Yellow Sheet, 1913, oil on canvas

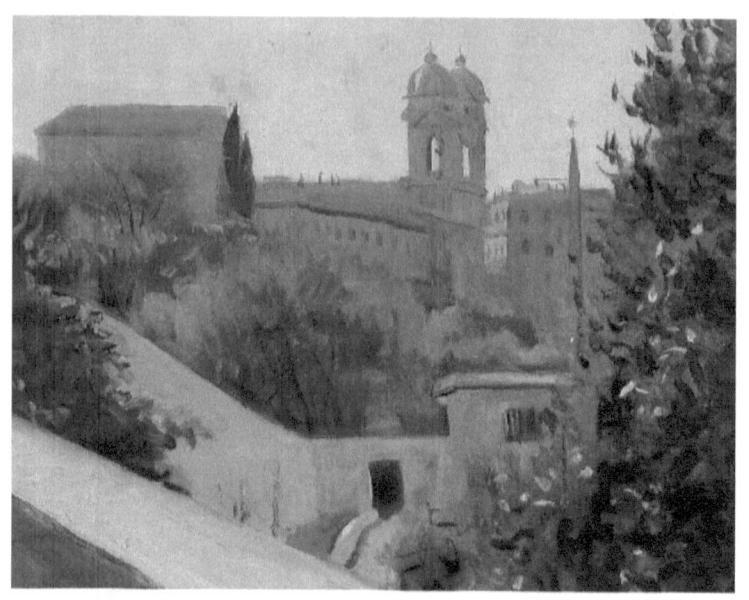

Trinity of the Mount, 1913, oil on canvas

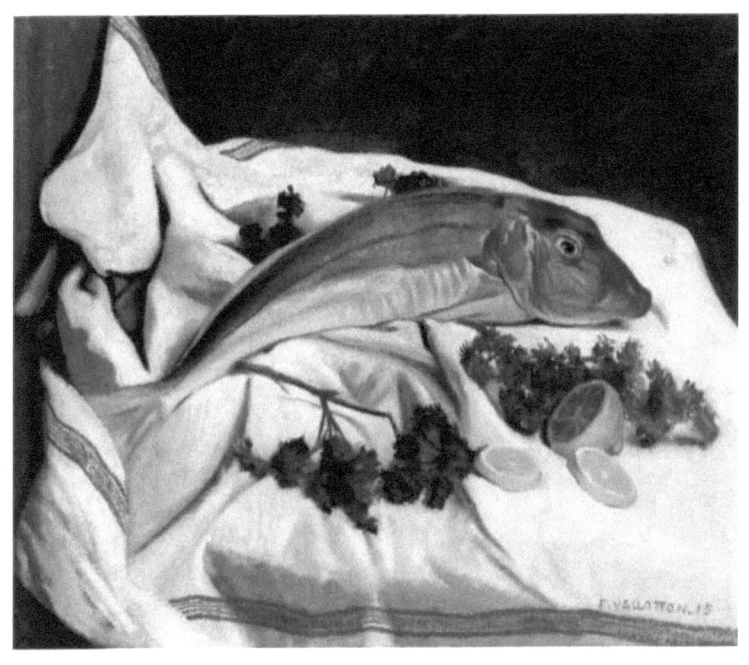

A Gurnard one has towel, 1914, oil on canvas

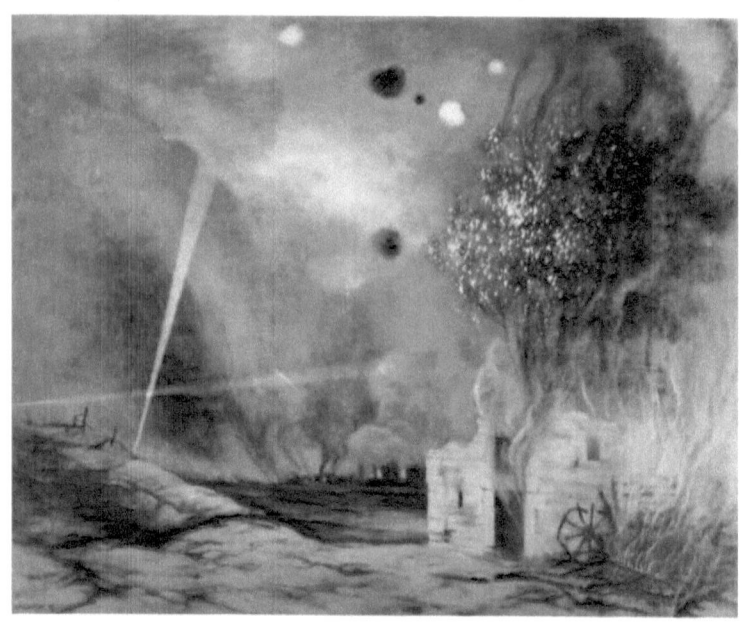

Landscape off ruins and fires, 1914, oil on canvas

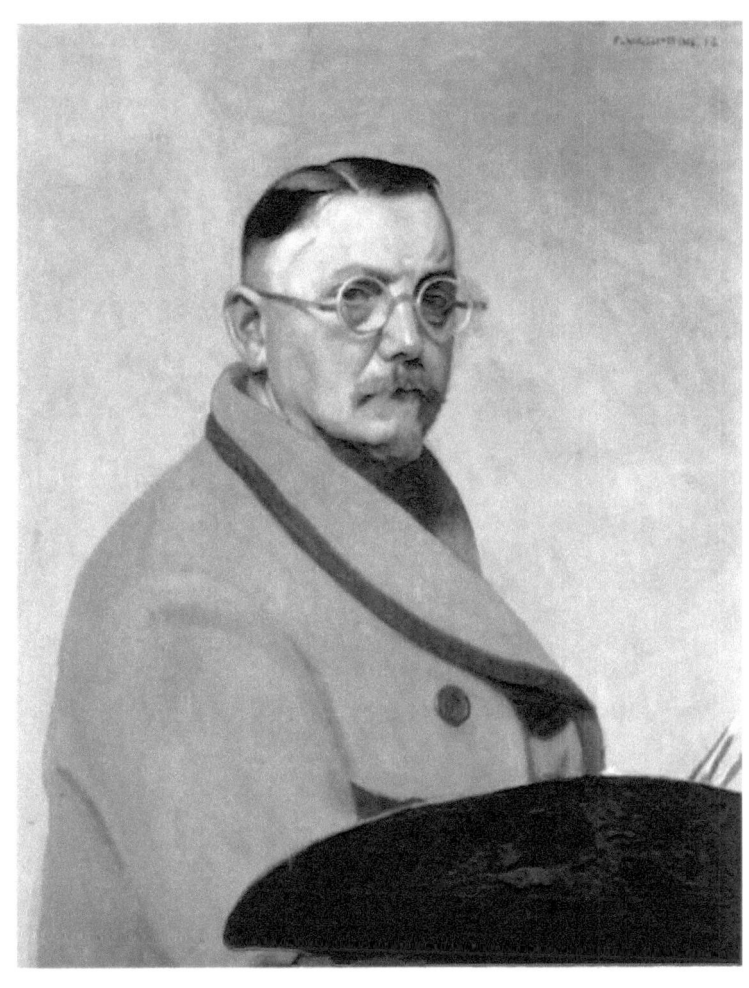

Self-portrait with the dressing gown, 1914, oil on canvas

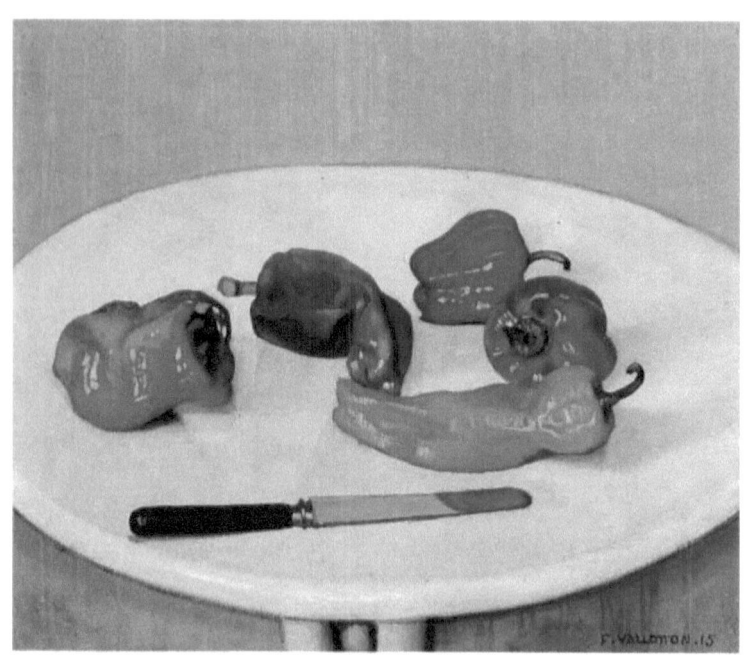

Still Life with Red Peppers on a White Lacquered
Table, 1915, oil on canvas

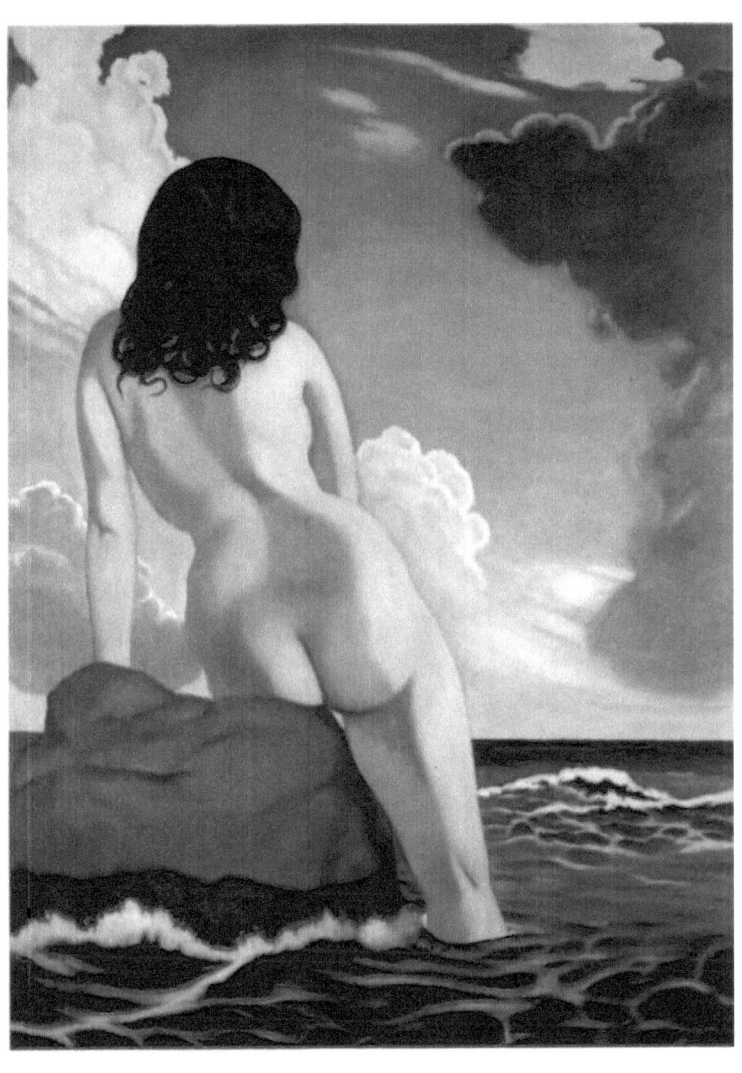

Bather, stormy sky, 1916, oil

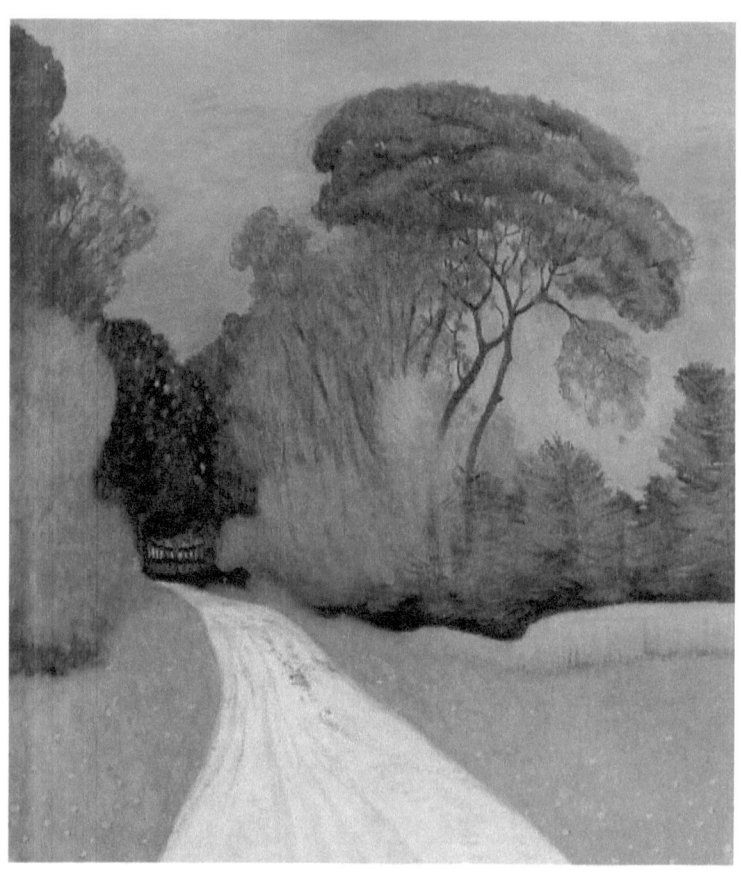

The Entrance to the Villa Beaulieu in Honfleur (also known as Before the Storm), 1916, oil on canvas

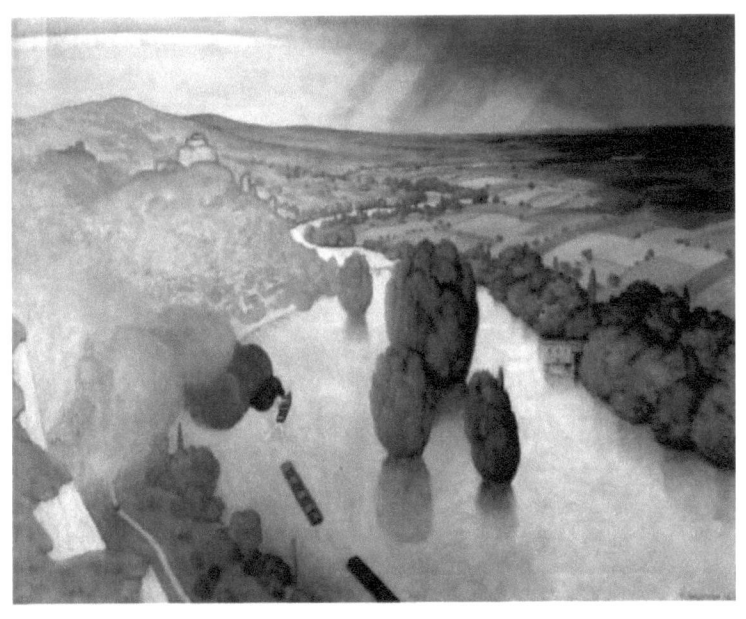

To remember Andelys, 1916, oil on canvas

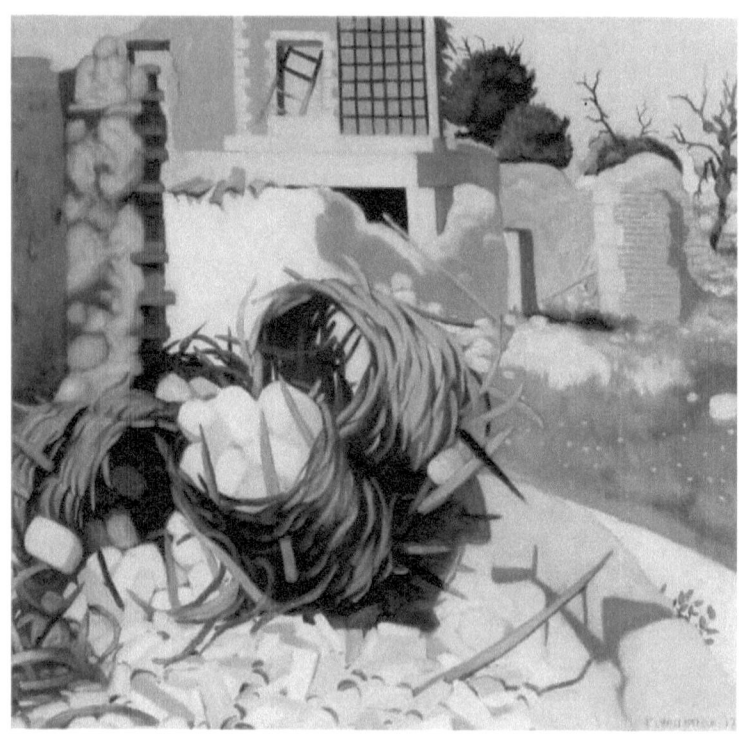

Ruins at Souain, 1917, oil on canvas

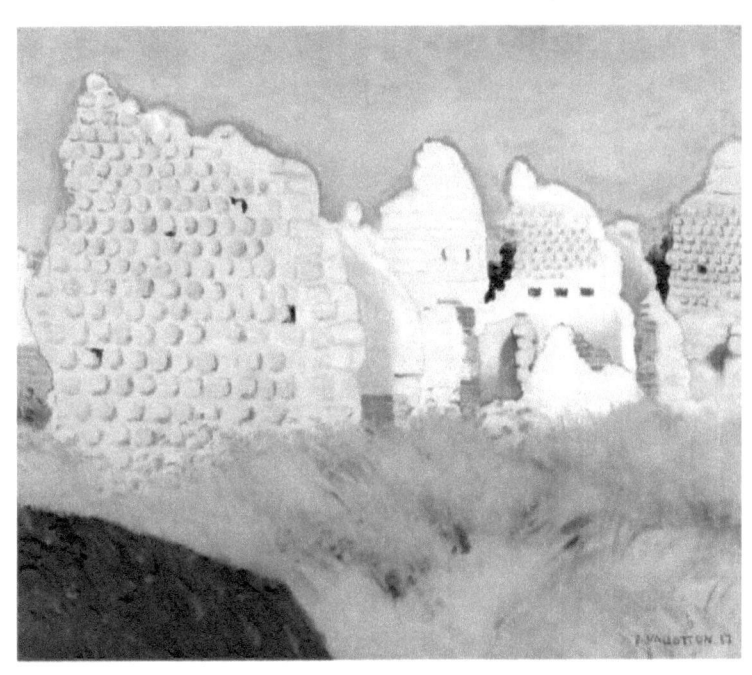

Ruins at Souain, Sunset, 1917, oil

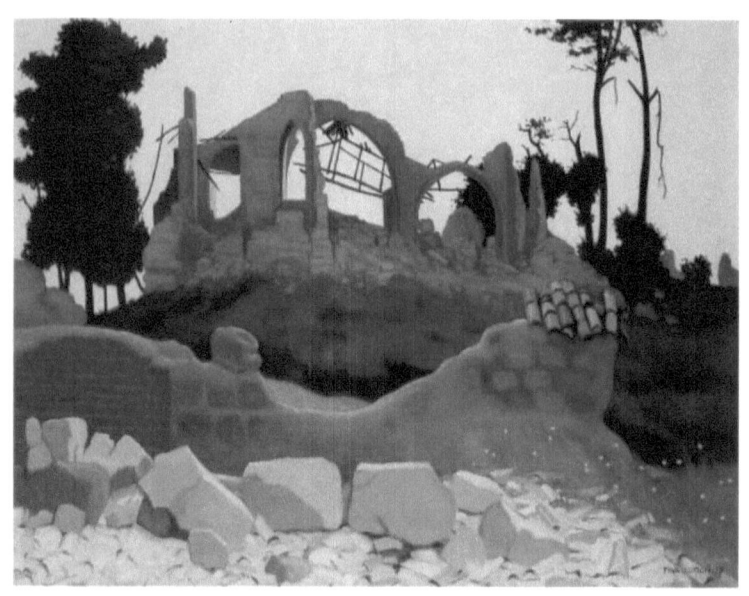

The Church of Souain in Sihlouette, 1917, oil

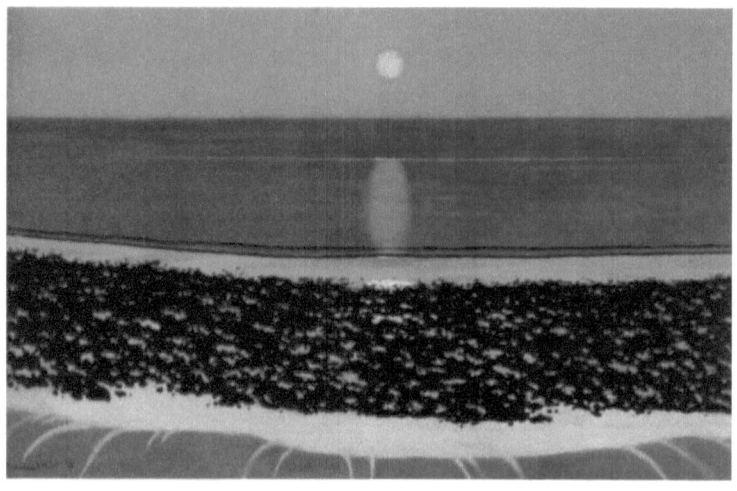

To lay down sun with Villerville, 1917, oil on canvas

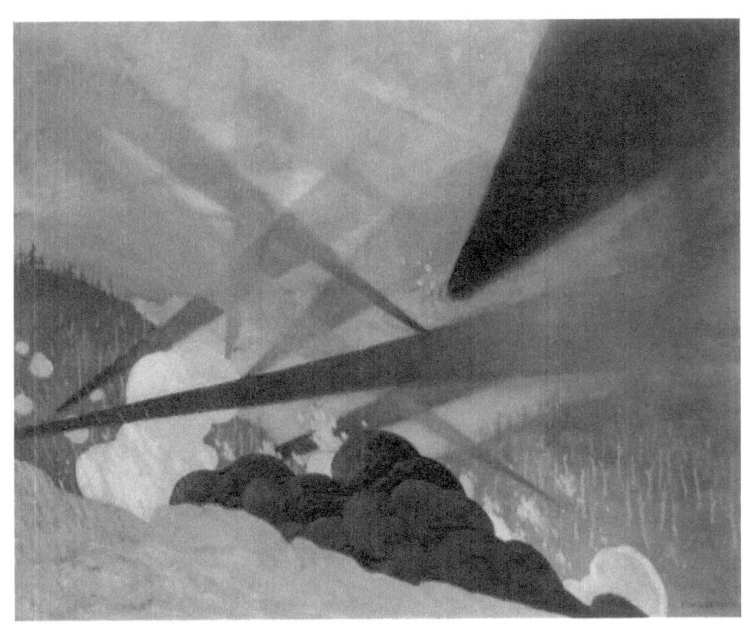

Verdun, 1917, oil on canvas

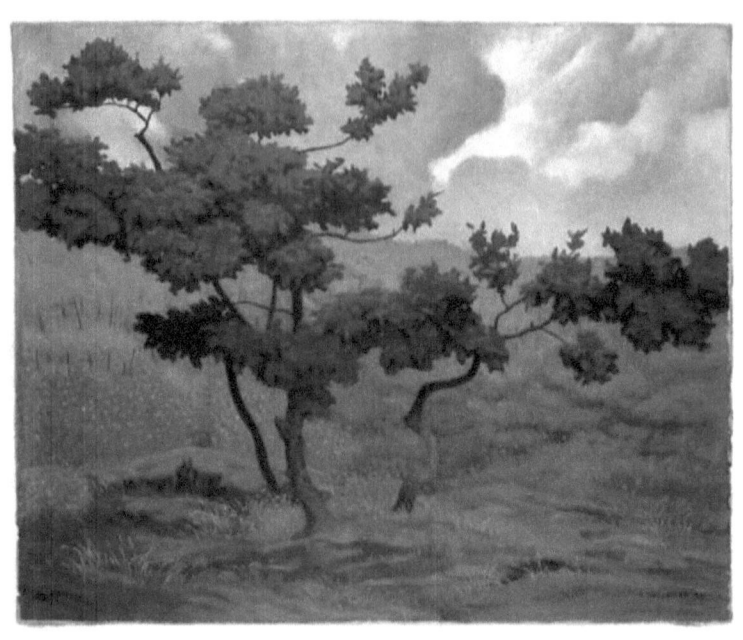

Landscape made in wood, 1918, oil

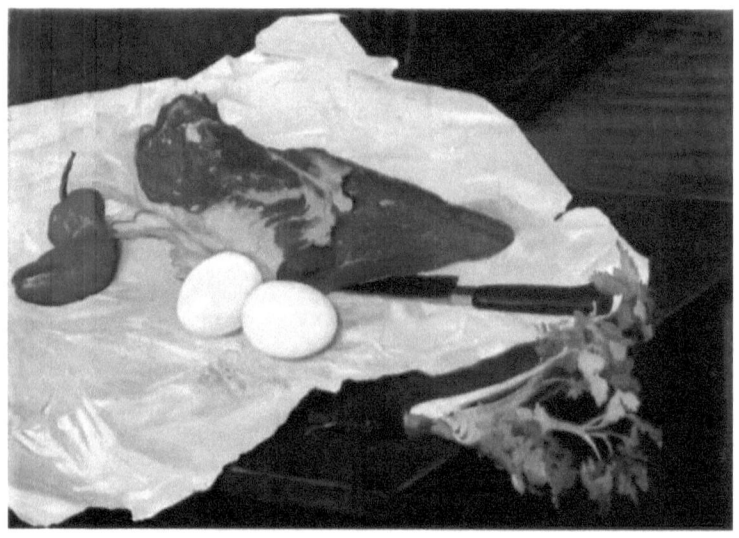

Meat and eggs, 1918, oil

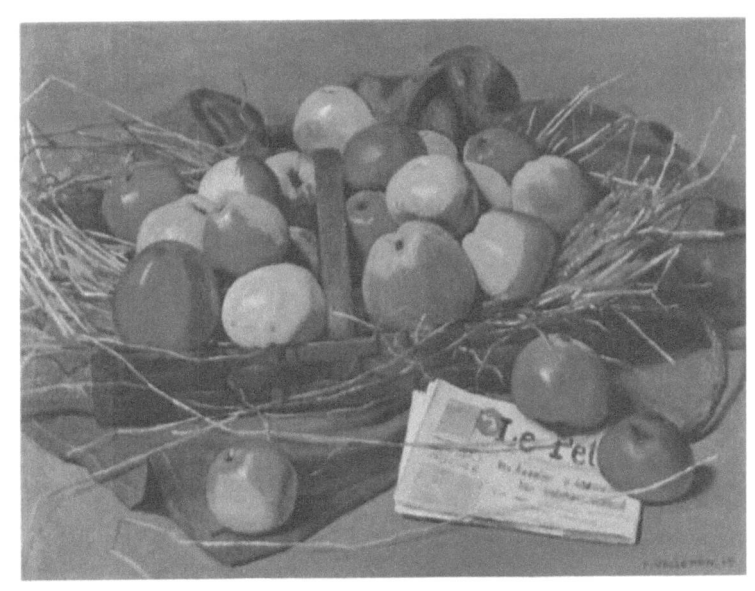

Apples, 1919, oil

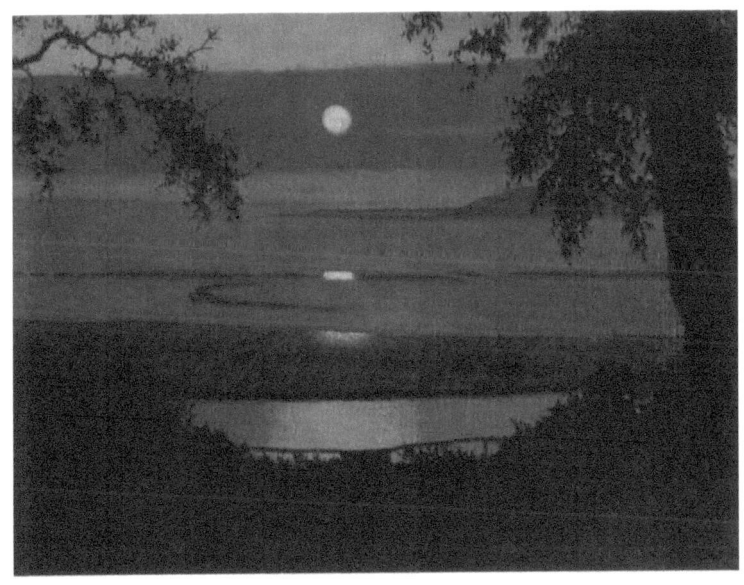

Sunset, 1918, oil on canvas

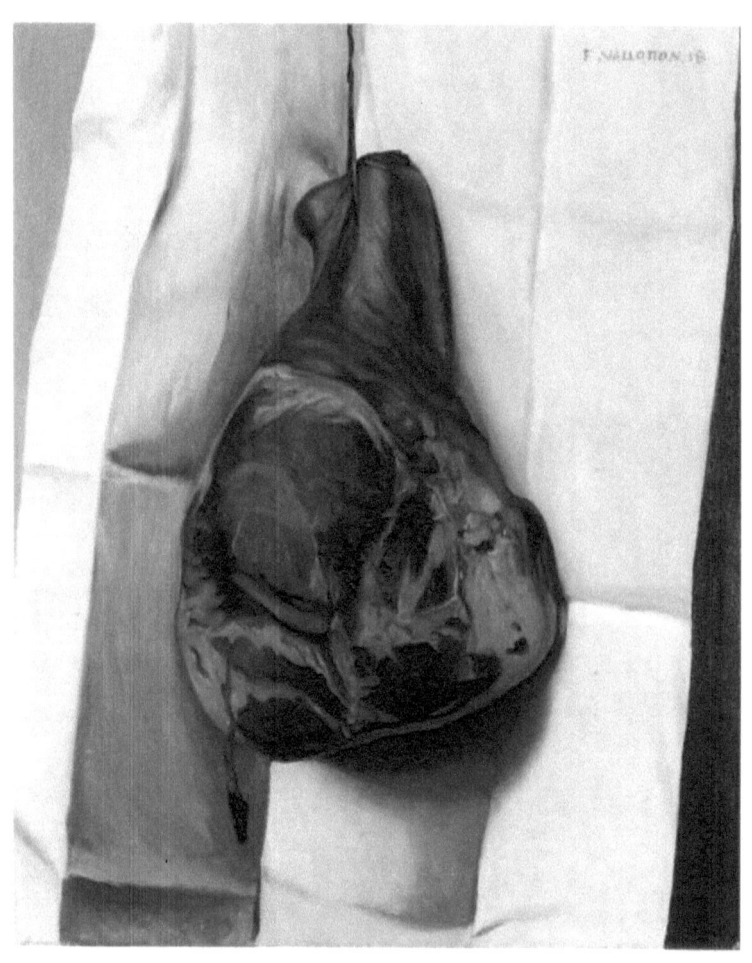

The Ham, 1918, oil

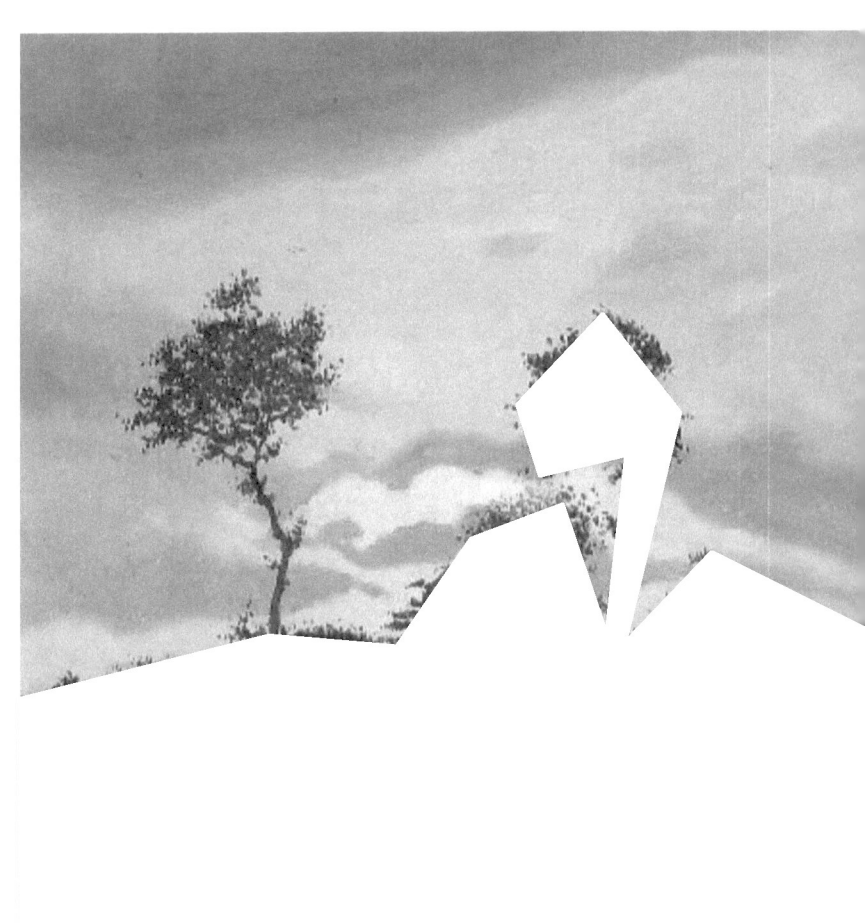

Landscape at Sunset, 1919, oil on canvas

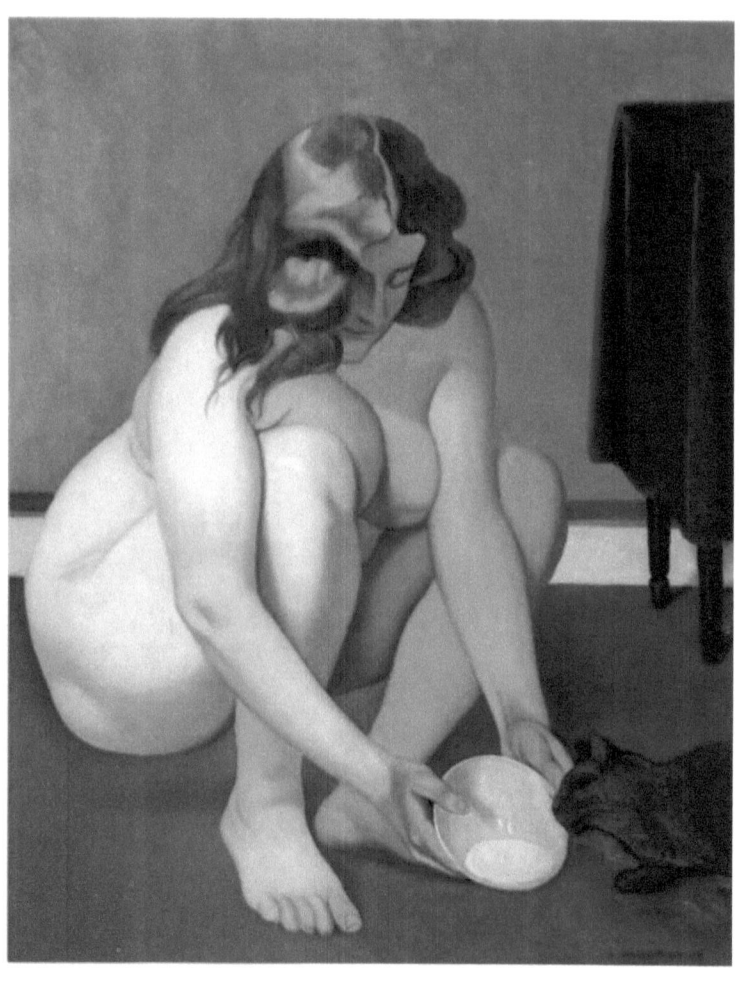

Squatted woman offering of milk to a cat, 1919, oil

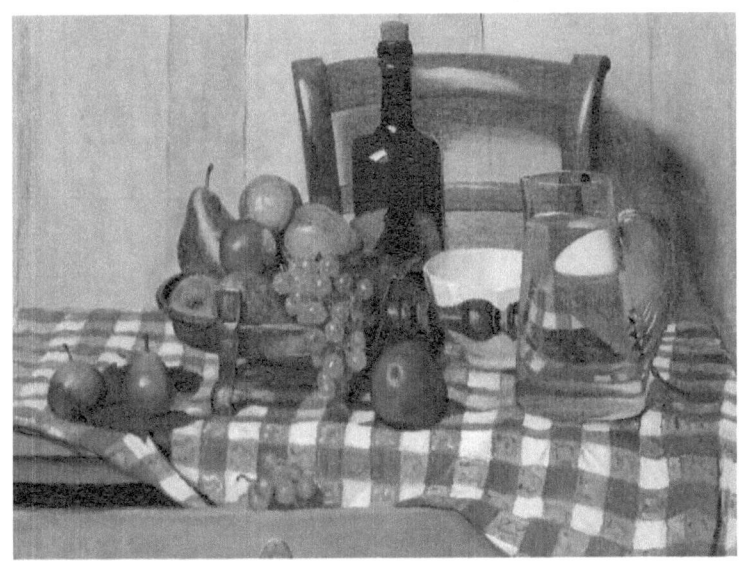

Still Life with Blue Checkered Tablecloth, 1919, oil on
canvas

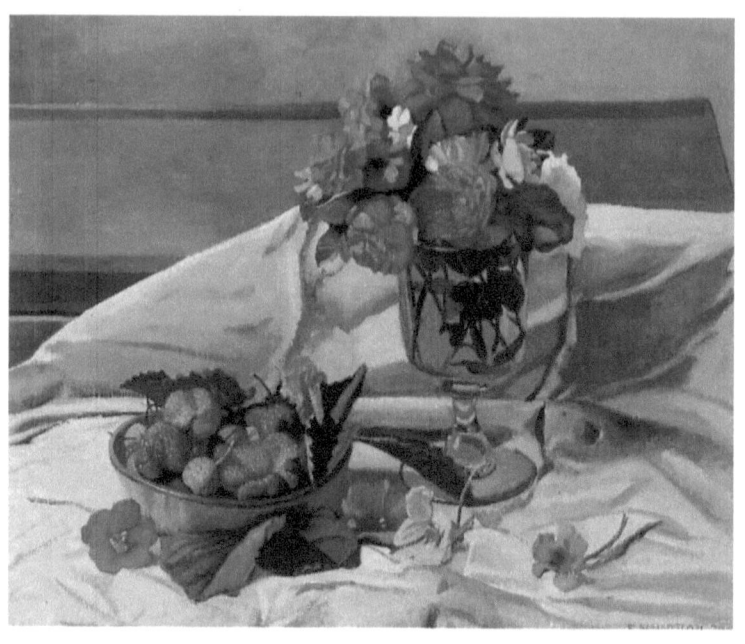

Flowers and Strawberries, 1920, oil on canvas

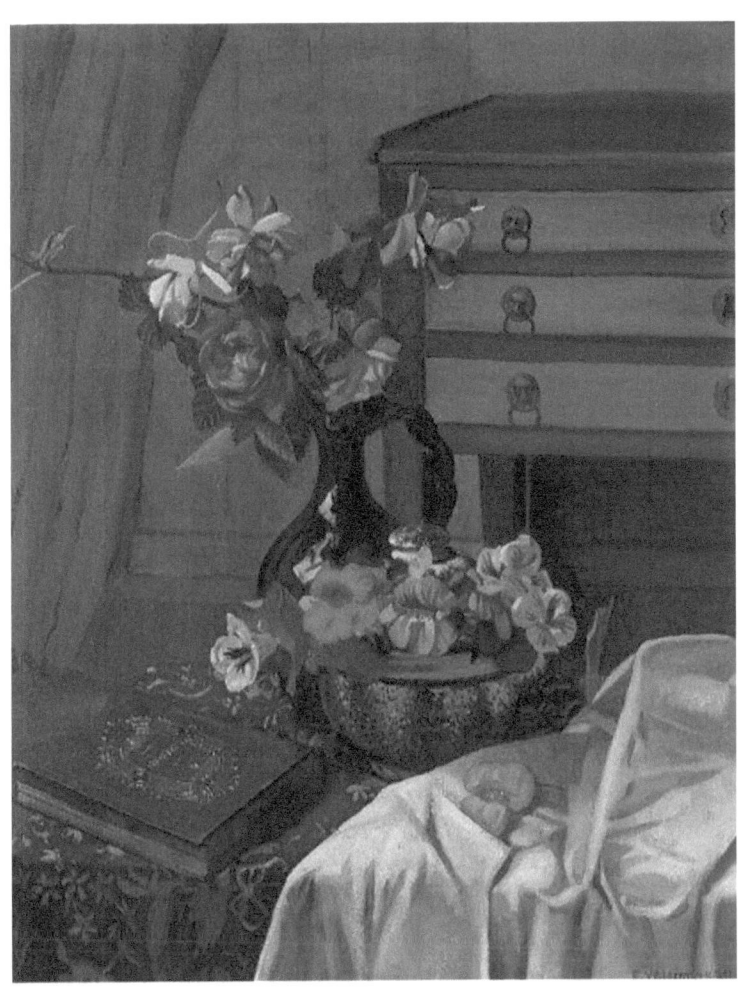

Roses and nasturtiums, 1920, oil

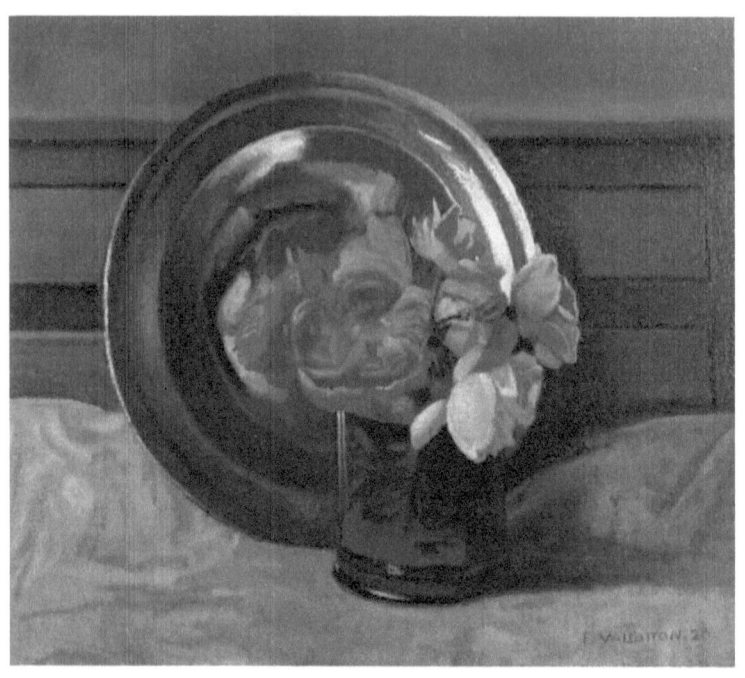

Still Life with Roses, 1920, oil

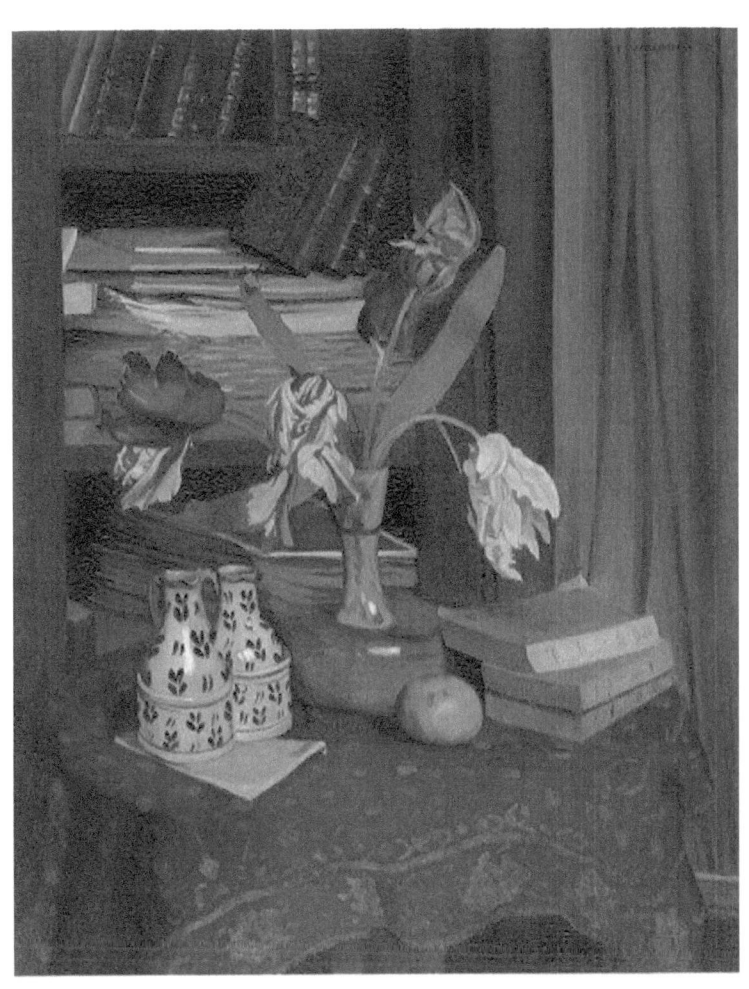

Tulipes perroquet, 1920, oil

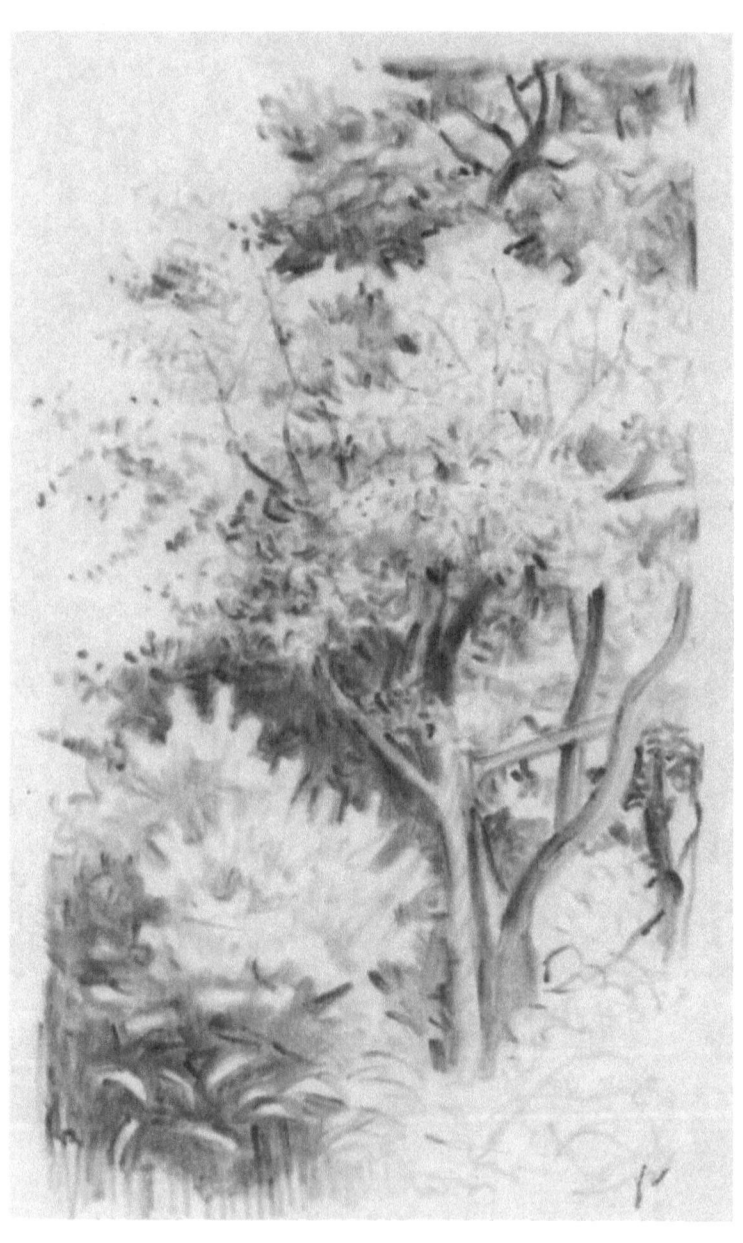

Wood
1920, drawing

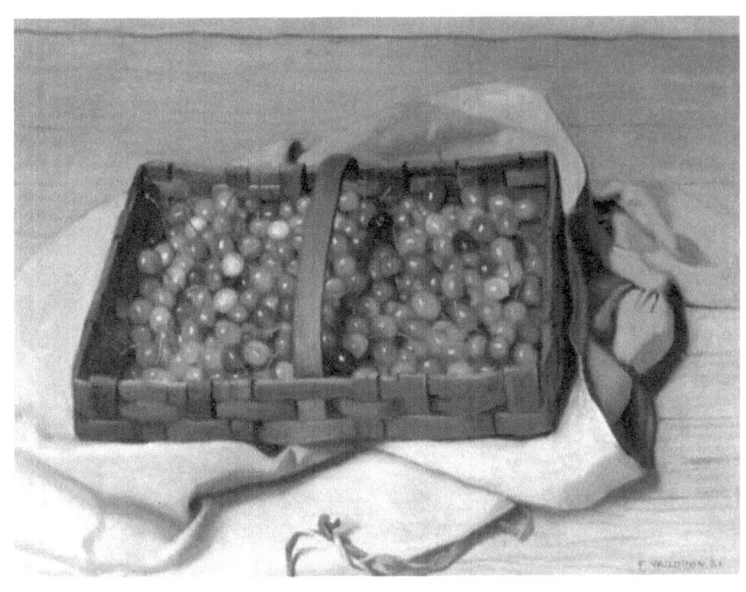

Basket of Cherries, 1921, oil on canvas

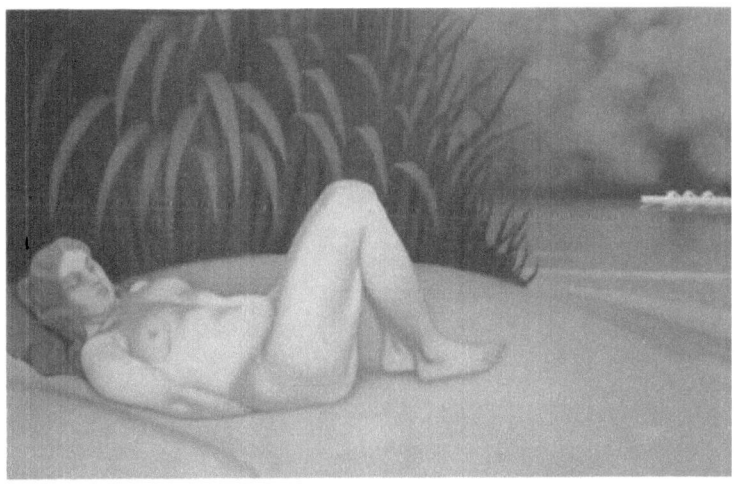

Naked woman sleeping at the edge of the water, 1921, oil

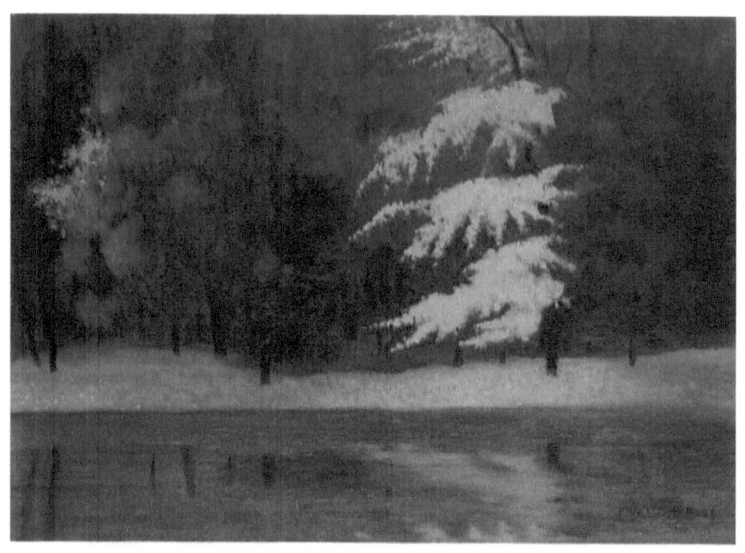

The Lake in the Bois de Boulogne, 1921, oil on canvas

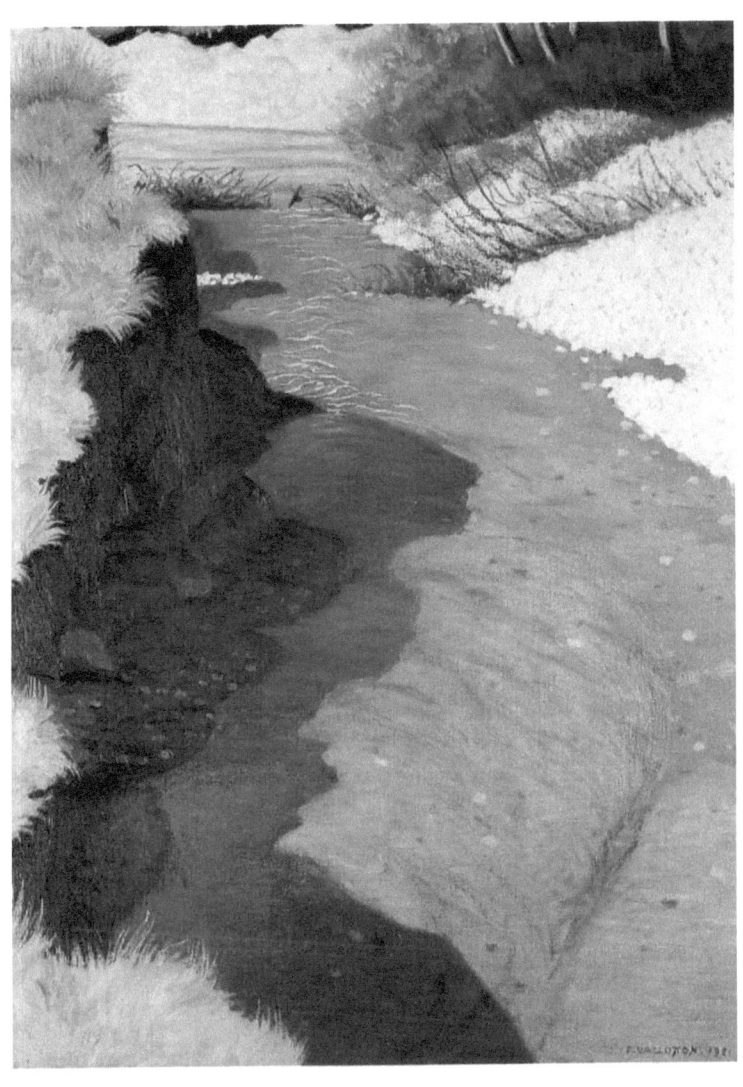

View of Cagne from Horseback, 1921, oil on canvas

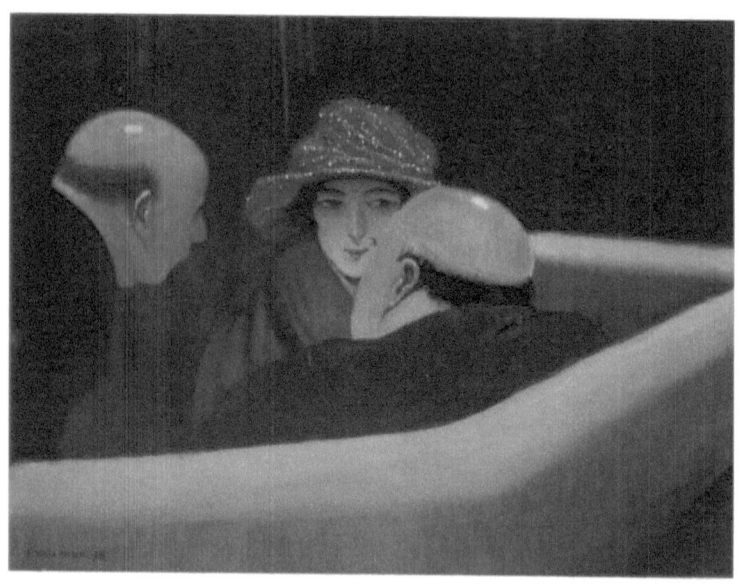

Chaste Suzanne, 1922, oil

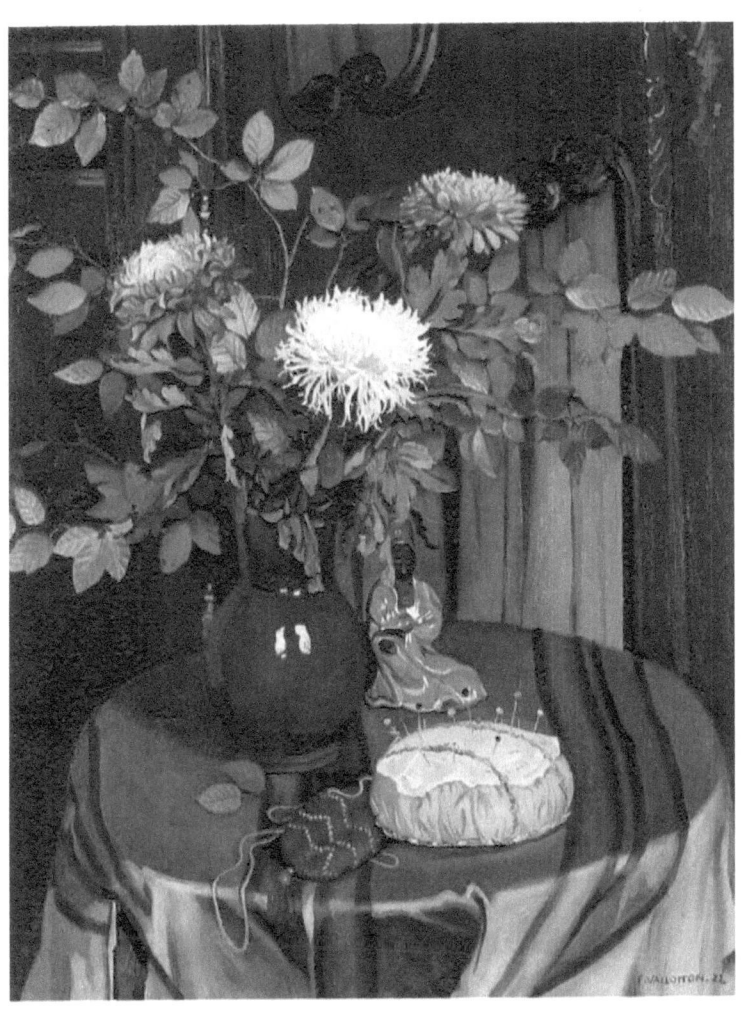

Chrysanthemums and Autumn Foliage, 1922, oil on canvas

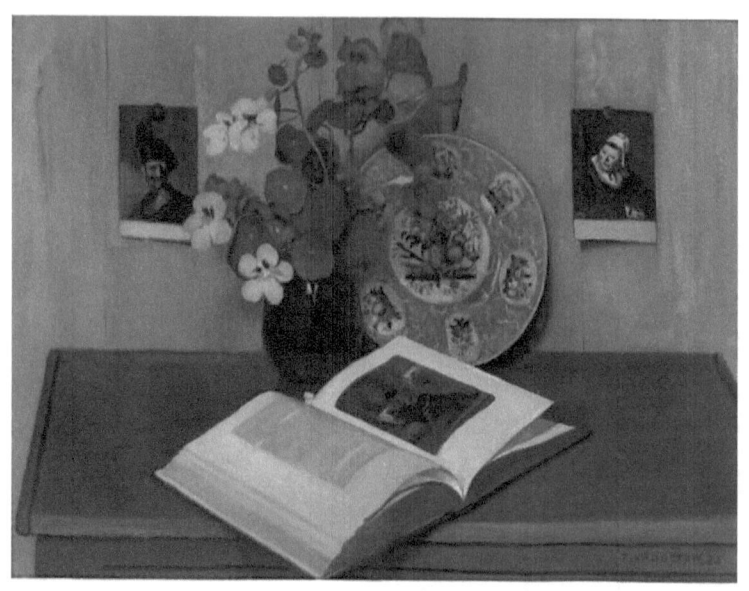

Still Life with Blue trim, 1922, oil

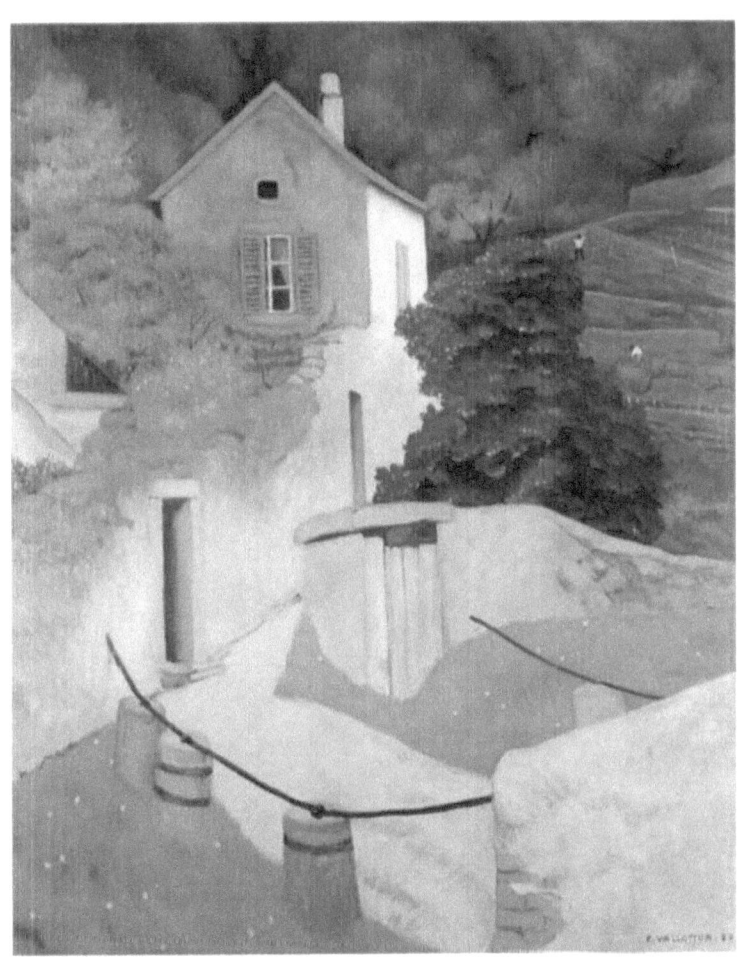

A Vallon Landscape, 1923, oil

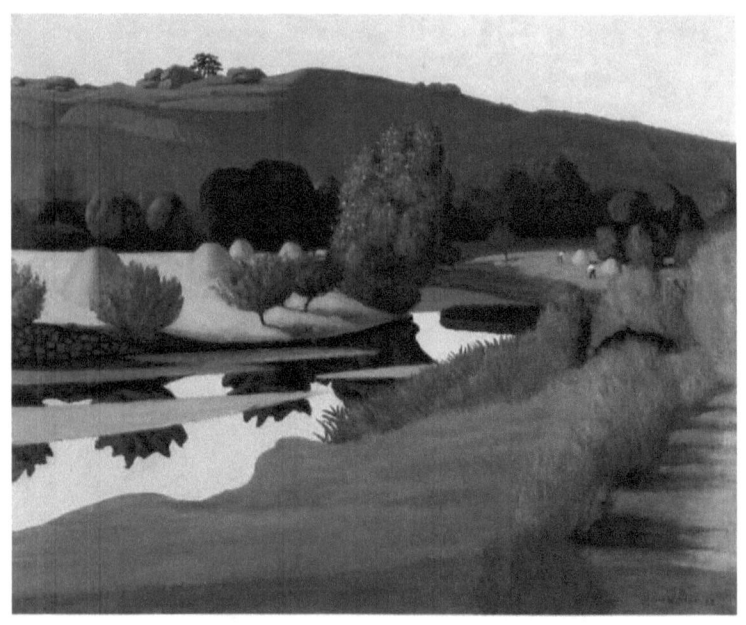

Evening on the Loire, 1923, oil on canvas

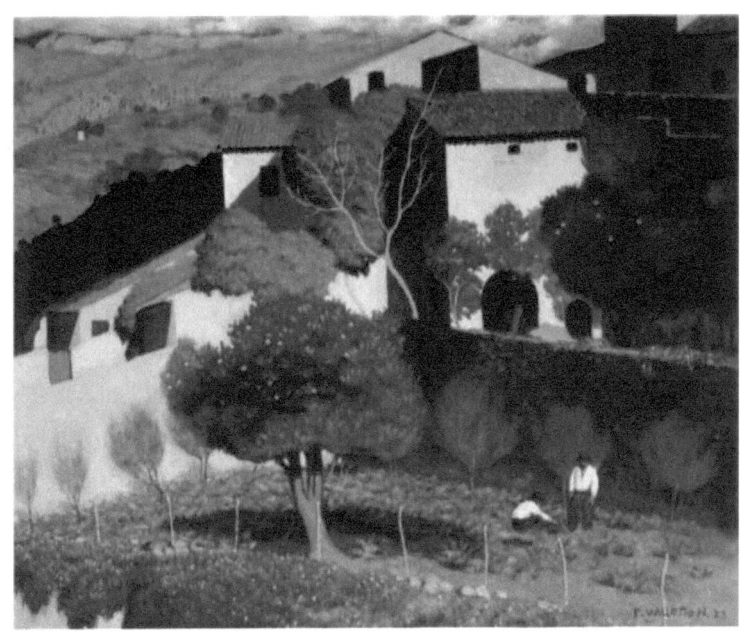

Landscape in Cagnes, 1923, oil

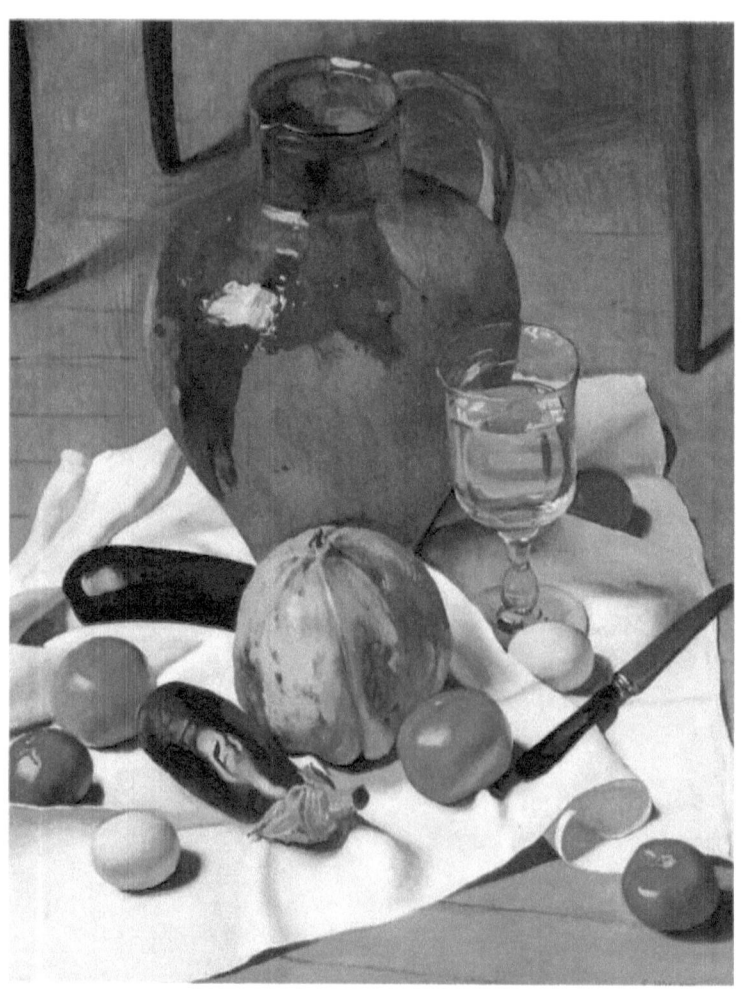

Still Life with Large Earthenware Jug, 1923, oil

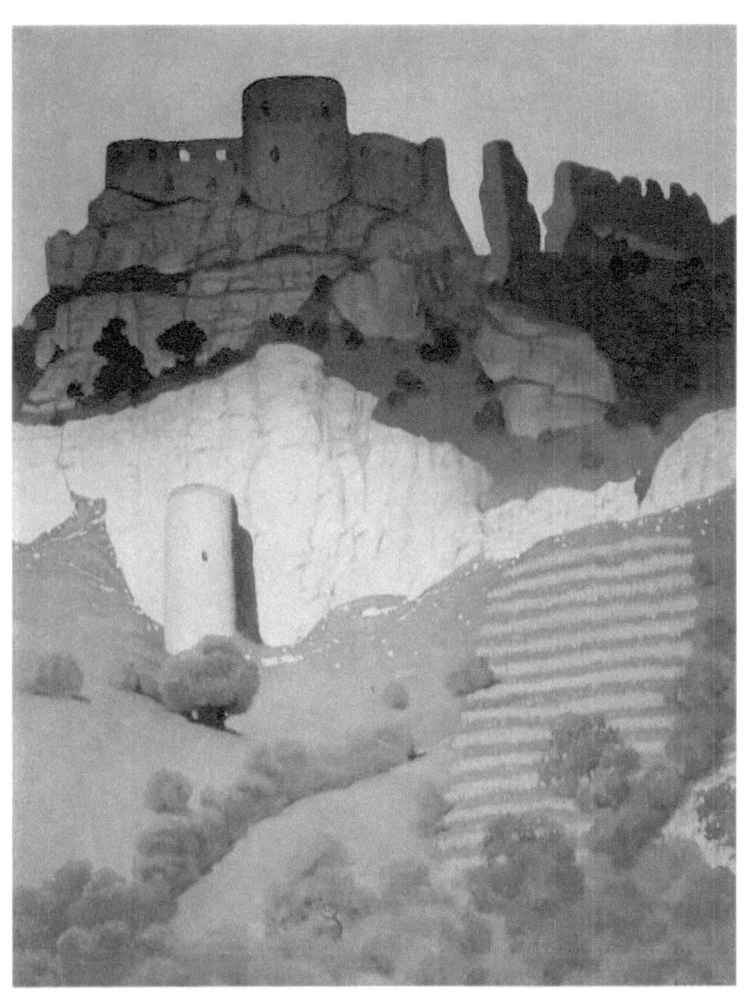

Chateau Gaillard at Andelys, 1924, oil

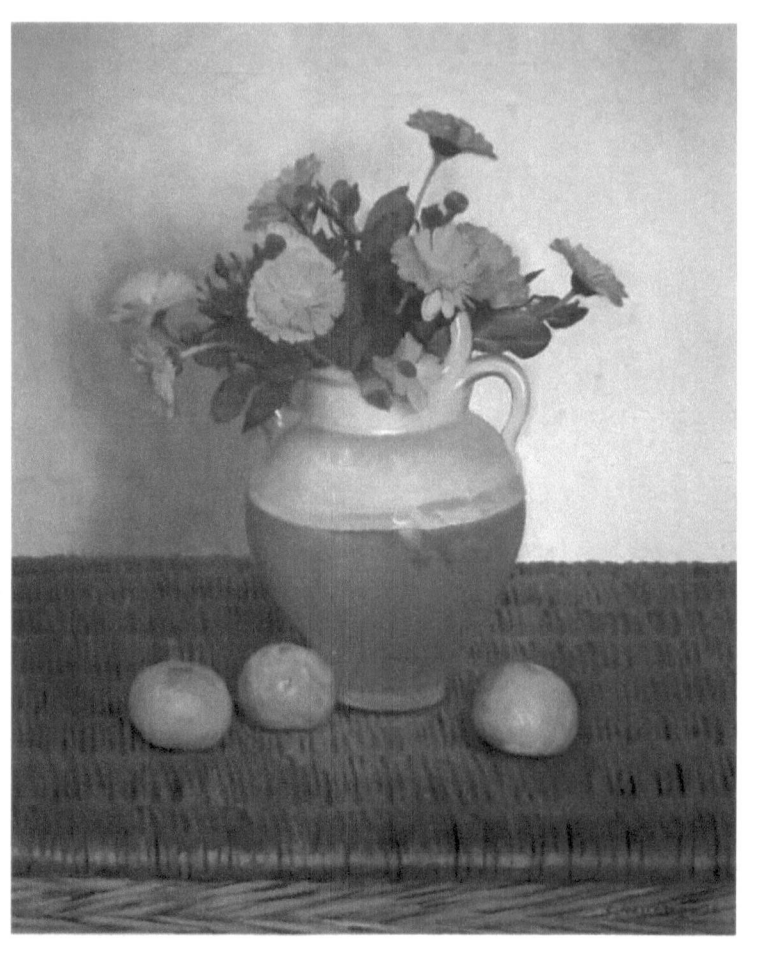

Marigolds and Tangerines, 1924, oil

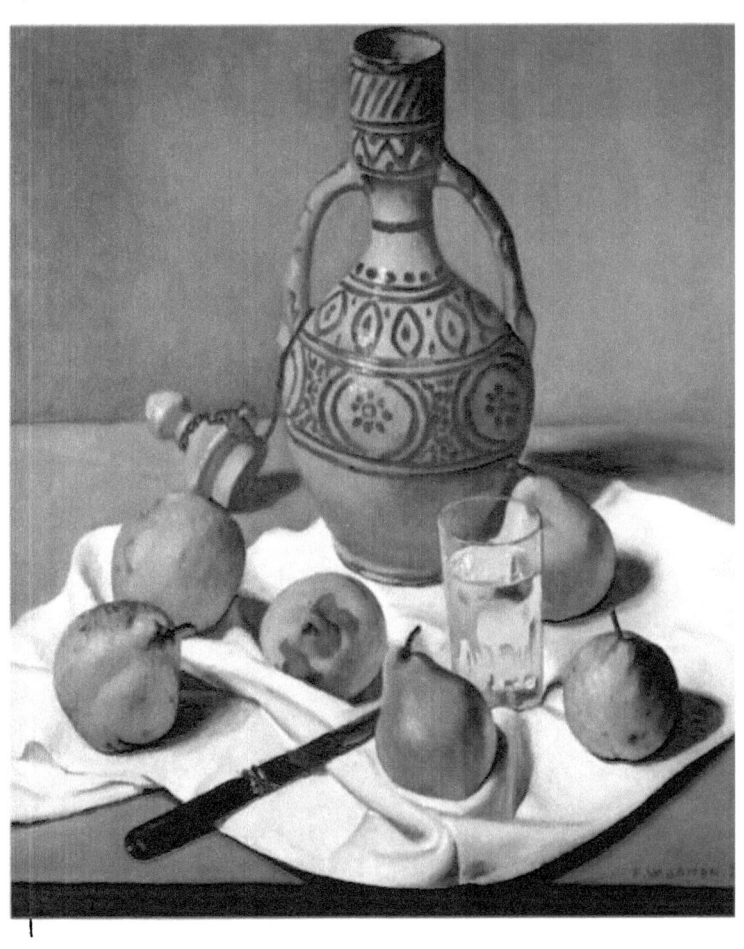

Moroccan jug and pears, 1924, oil

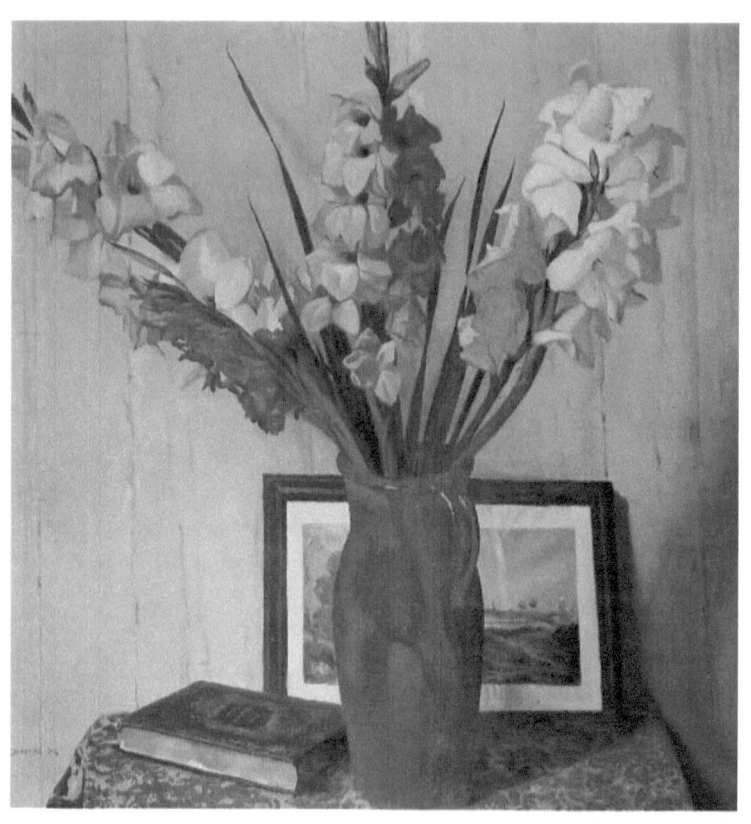

Still Life with Gladioli, 1924, oil on canvas

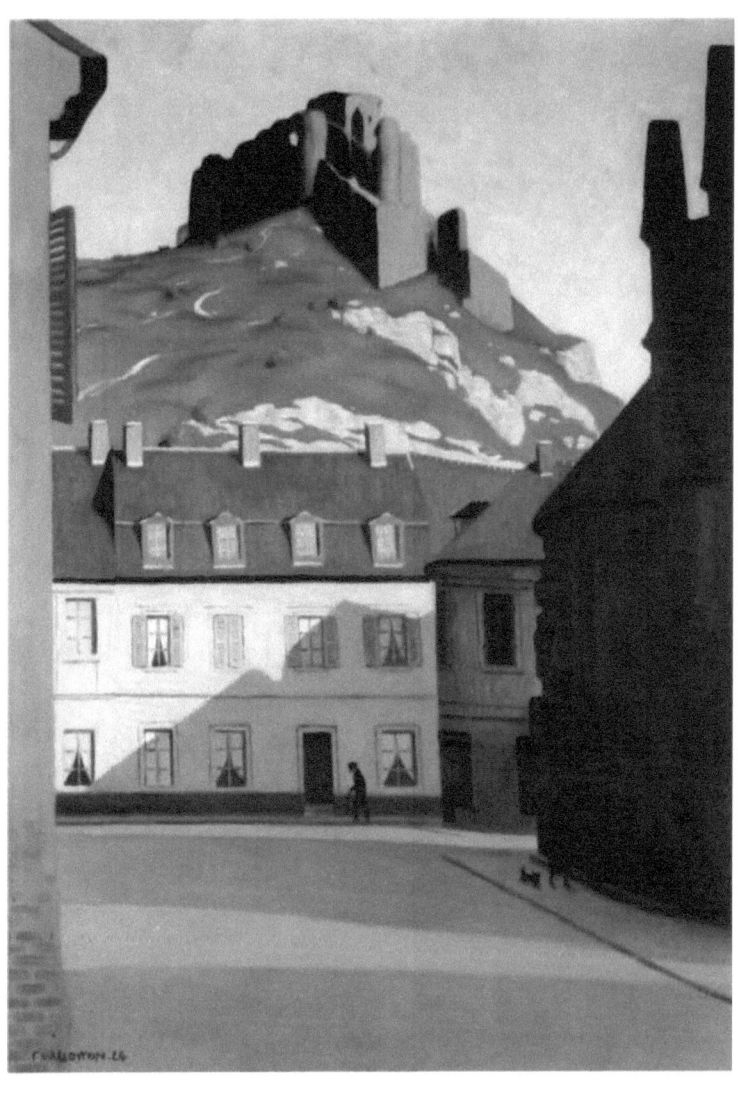

The Strong Castle and the place of Andelys, 1924, oil

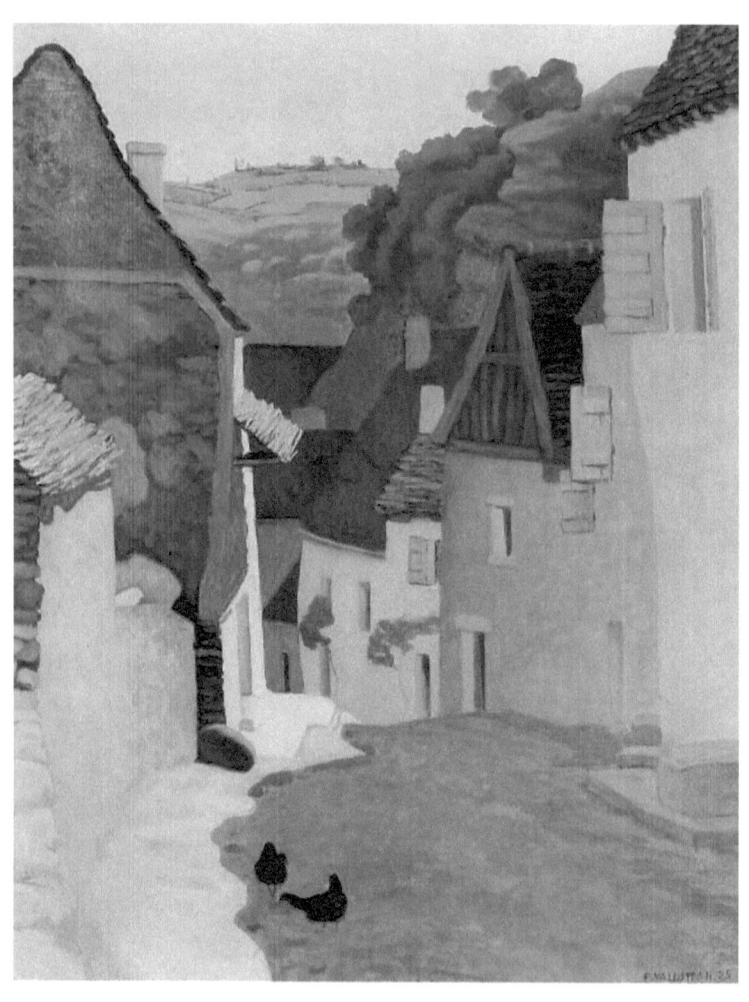

Rocamadour Landscape, 1925, oil on canvas

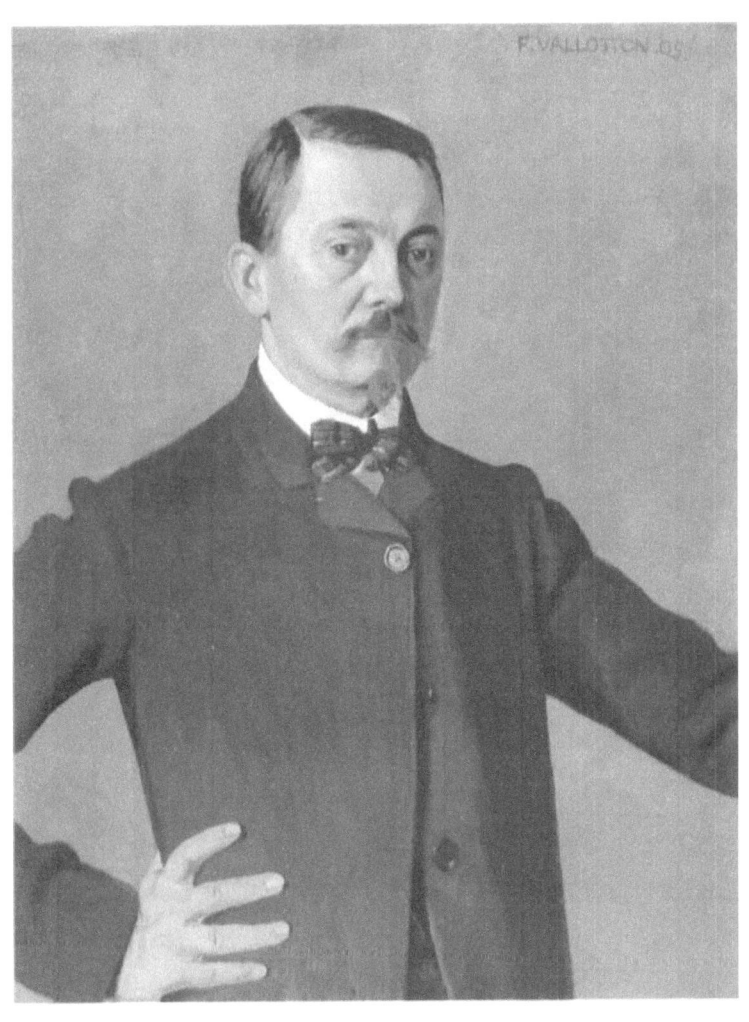

Self-portrait, 1925, oil on canvas

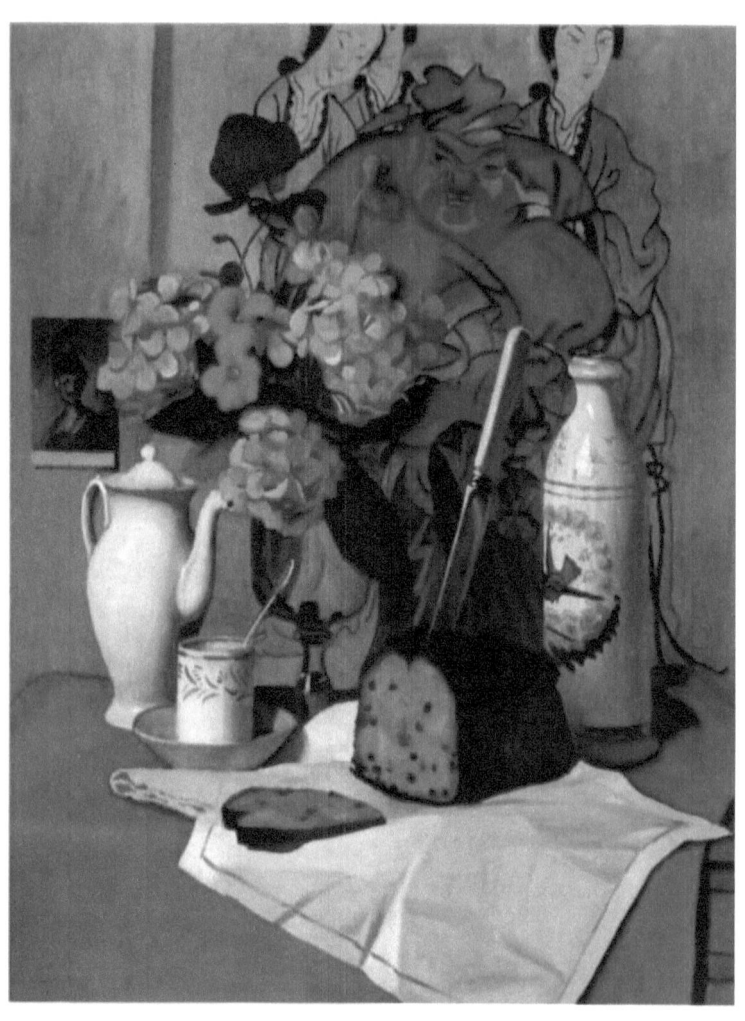

Still life in Chinese painting, 1925, oil on canvas

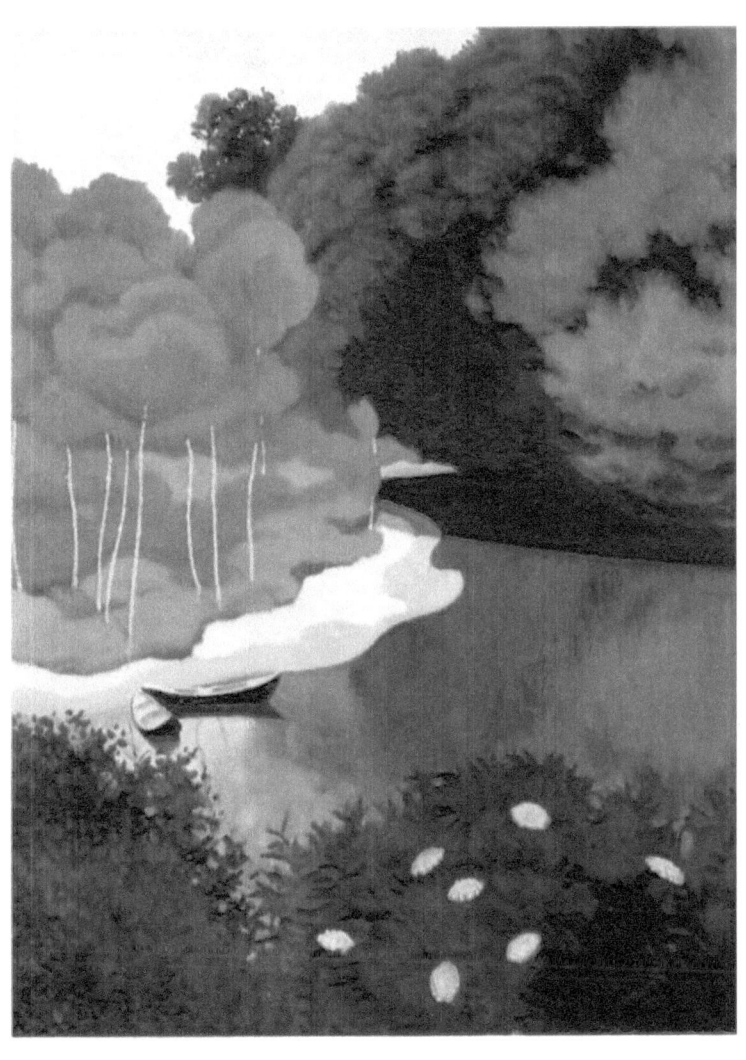

At the Beach, 1925, oil

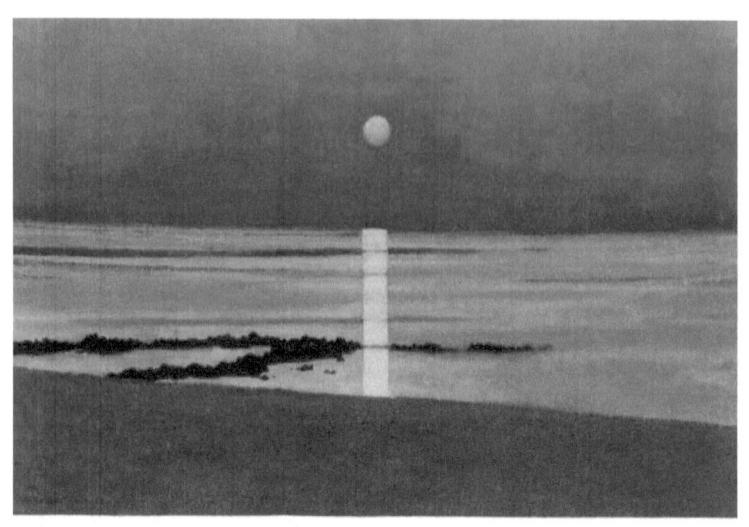

Sunset, oil on canvas